A Piece of My M

Dramatist Peter Nichols has often plundered episodes in his own life to provide the subject matter of his plays. In his latest, *A Piece of My Mind* he has gone one stage further, transforming a self-confessed case of writer's block into a continuously inventive and thought-provoking comedy.

Like Nichols himself, his hero, Ted Forrest, is a playwright who has turned his back on the theatre and retired to the country to write a novel. Like Nichols he is finding it a damnably difficult business. And like Nichols, he turns his struggles into a drama about his own life and the process of artistic creation.

All this might easily have been a monumental exercise in self-indulgence, but Nichols scarcely puts a foot wrong. There is much self mockery, irony is piled upon irony and the many jokes are almost all excellent.

There are gags about the theatre, with the actors stepping out of their scenes to comment on the proceedings, or challenge what the author has written about them. The theatre critics come in for a stream of virulently entertaining abuse as the dramatist trots out the cliché-ridden notices of the past and the play also has much to say on that old chestnut, the nature of illusion and reality.

But *A Piece of My Mind* is more than an effervescent jeu d'esprit. Though the style is oblique and playful, this is a surprisingly moving evening. It would be impertinent to speculate on just how much Nichols resembles Ted Forrest. But the character's self doubt and jealousy . . . and the portrait of a marriage and his strained relationship with his teenage children all seem to come straight from the heart. They are all the more affecting for being described within the context of such immaculate artifice.

Charles Spencer, *London Daily News*

PETER NICHOLS was born in Bristol in 1927 and went to Bristol Grammar School. When the war ended, he did National Service with the RAF in India and the Far East. He then studied at the Bristol Old Vic Theatre School and was an actor for five years. He later taught in London schools. He has written over twenty plays for television, several feature film scripts and the following stage plays: *A Day in the Death of Joe Egg* (1967) and *The National Health* (1969) both winners of the Evening Standard Best Play Award; *Forget-Me-Not Lane* (1971); *Chez Nous* (1974); *The Freeway* (1974); *Privates on Parade* (1977), which won Best Comedy Awards from the Evening Standard and SWET and the Ivor Novello Award for Best British Musical; *Born in the Gardens* (1979); *Passion Play* (1981); and *Poppy* (1982), which got the SWET Award for Best British Musical. He was resident playwright at the Guthrie, Minneapolis, where he co-directed *The National Health*. He also directed a *Joe Egg* revival at Greenwich and the first *Born in the Gardens* at Bristol. *Feeling You're Behind*, an autobiography, came out in 1984.

PETER NICHOLS

A Piece of My Mind

A Methuen Paperback

A METHUEN MODERN PLAY

First published in Great Britain in 1987 as a Methuen Paperback original
by Methuen London Ltd, 11 New Fetter Lane, London EC4P 4EE
and in the United States of America by Methuen Inc,
29 West 35th Street, New York, NY 10001.

British Library Cataloguing in Publication Data

Nichols, Peter, *1927*—
    A piece of my mind. — (A Methuen
    modern play).
    I. Title
    822'.914   PR6064.12

    ISBN 0-413-17360-7

**To Charles and Valerie Wood
– still friends**

And when I die, my friends, as they pass by my grave, will say:
'Here lies Trigorin. He was a good writer, but not as good
as Turgenev.'

Chekhov: *The Seagull*.

Don't get complicated. You get complicated, you get sad. You
get sad, your luck goes.

Raymond Chandler: Film: *The Blue Dahlia*.

The first production of *A Piece of My Mind* opened in London at the Apollo Theatre on 1 April 1987. Prior to that it had been seen in Southampton, Croydon, Brighton, Bath, York and Richmond. The cast for all venues was as follows:

TED FORREST, 50s   George Cole

DINAH FORREST
NANCY FRASER   } ACTRESS ONE 40+ Anna Carteret
A MARCHIONESS
A NURSING SISTER

A CRITIC
CHARLES UPCRAFT   } ACTOR ONE 40+   Jerome Willis
WALTER FORREST
A VICAR

BECKY FORREST
UPCRAFT'S
  SECRETARY
APRIL   } ACTRESS TWO 20+ Gwyneth Strong
MAI
JUNE
AN AWARDS
  PRESENTER

TOM FORREST
AN OLD SALT
MILES WHITTIER   } ACTOR TWO 20+   Patrick Pearson
SPEED
A HOSPITAL
  ORDERLY

Directed by Justin Greene

ACT ONE

The assembling audience faces a bird's-eye view of a manor house in the English countryside. Perhaps a painting or photograph but in any case an image that represents a sort of perfection. Though, centuries ago, it began as symmetrical, the tastes of its various occupiers and the necessities of farming, stabling, gardening and garaging have surrounded it with outbuildings. Its stone is mellow, with wistaria and creeper clambering across its walls and mature trees clustering round.

We draw closer by degrees, each picture on the scrim taking us a little nearer, as a windhover might on a fine day. The sound of animals, birds, bees, power-saws, church bells, tractors; but the bleating of sheep finally predominates. At last we've closed on one window, so that the picture image is the same size as the room behind, as we see when the lights go up on the set. The scrim is flown out.

The room's a study, with a large modern desk about centre stage. The general impression is of ordered comfort, some furniture old, even antique, some new and functional.

Three people are present. ACTOR ONE, *middle-aged and wearing a lounge suit, stands by the wall, right, holding open the lid of an ottoman, roughly the size of a coffin.* ACTOR TWO, *in his 20s and wearing expensive casuals, is near him, looking down into the box.* ACTRESS TWO *stands by the central desk, wearing a nurse's uniform and watching* ACTOR TWO. *The actress is in her early 20s.*

A church bells tolls.

ACTOR TWO. A tragic loss.

ACTOR ONE. He was far too young to go, just like that.

ACTOR TWO. And always so good to me.

ACTOR ONE. It can't have been easy not to envy your success. But I knew you'd want to keep his memory green.

ACTOR TWO. Anything I can do, of course.

ACTOR ONE. I'm afraid the work of his we have won't ensure his survival.

ACTOR TWO. And you didn't find any new writing on his desk?

He turns to the ACTRESS *as* ACTOR ONE *closes the box lid.*

ACTRESS TWO. I thought he'd finished a novel but there's nothing.

ACTOR ONE. No plays, no stories, no sketches?

ACTRESS TWO. None.

ACTOR ONE. So if you could knock out something in his style it would be such a kindness to his widow here. You've met, of course? Miles Whittier.

ACTRESS TWO. Oh, yes, we've met.

She moves to meet ACTOR TWO, *who embraces her.*

ACTOR TWO. I'll help in any way I can, of course.

ACTRESS TWO. And I'll help *you* in any way *I* can.

She kisses him ardently. They feel each other up.

I've wanted to for years.

ACTOR TWO. Did he guess?

ACTRESS TWO. Never for a second.

As she leads him towards the desk and sits on its edge, raising her legs to him, there's a drumming from the ottoman. ACTOR ONE *crosses to them.*

ACTOR ONE. Just a minute. Write the play first, enjoy yourselves later. No need to behave like animals.

ACTOR TWO *has raised her skirt to show her thighs in black stockings.* ACTOR ONE *pulls* ACTOR TWO *away.*
   ACTOR TWO *sits at the desk, looking down at an old portable typewriter with a sheet of paper in the roll. Then knocking and some faint cries come from the ottoman.* ACTRESS TWO *goes to sit on the upstage desk edge, her back to us.*

ACTOR TWO. Now let me see. Act One, Scene One.

He types this, while the others watch spellbound.

ACTOR ONE. Marvellous. You've caught his tone exactly.

ACTRESS TWO. This will be my late husband's masterpiece. Put your hand up my skirt if it helps.

He does. She whimpers with delight.

ACTOR ONE. You always were a master of pastiche.

ACTRESS TWO. Among so many other skills.

More knocking on the box. The lid is pushed up an inch or two but falls back. Then again a bit further. Feeble groans from there.

ACTOR ONE (*goes to ram down the lid*). Too late, you've had your chance.

Another cry from inside. He sits on it to hold it down.

ACTOR TWO. It will all take place in the writer's study.

ACTRESS TWO ⎱ (*together*). Brilliant!
ACTOR ONE ⎰

ACTOR ONE. I'm afraid I can't hold him down.

ACTOR TWO *types again. More knocking.*
All three now go off by the nearest door; the knocking, typing and cries continue.
Lights up on the room, much brighter. The room appears to be unoccupied. The knocking's different, coming from a door on the left of the upstage wall. Someone tries to turn the knob.

DINAH (*off*). Ted!

An easy chair, which had been turned from us, now pivots to reveal TED waking with a start; middle-aged, comfortably dressed.

TED. What? Hullo, what is it?

DINAH (*off*). Coffee.

He crosses to the audio set on a unit on the left wall under the bookshelves. He turns off the tape-recording of the typewriter then opens the door to let in DINAH, carrying a mug and a parcel.

Why is the door locked?

TED. I don't want the children wandering in here, breaking the mood.

DINAH. They don't arrive till this afternoon.

TED. Ah. (*He takes the parcel.*) What's this?

DINAH. A book, I should think, wouldn't you? From America. Came by second post.

He opens it with a paper knife. She takes binoculars from the desk and looks over the audience.

Those sheep look famished, there's nothing to graze on. And those pheasants better not start on my gooseberries again. Last year they had the lot. D'you think there'll be any quince? Remember how you used to like them poached with brown sugar, lemon juice and a pinch of cinnamon?

TED. Oh, Christ!

He has opened the parcel to find a thick dictionary sort of book.

DINAH (*puts down the glasses*). What is it?

TED. The Universal Writers' Biography. From Minnesota University. I fear the worst.

DINAH. I thought it was one of your military histories, else I'd never have let you have it. I'll take it away and make sure you're in there. If not, it can go out with the jumble.

TED. I'll be in there all right. I'm always in *this* one. It's what they'll say that worries me. I'm afraid they might have . . . yes, they *have*.

He has found his entry and now reads it.

'Edward Robert Forrest, born Birmingham, England, September 25th, 1930. Died April 1st, 1983.'

He looks at her.

DINAH. What? It says you're dead?

TED. 'Married Dinah Margaret Fletcher; one daughter, one son. During his all-too-short lifetime, Forrest impressed himself on the English-speaking theatre as a dramatist of unique and sometimes startling ability.'

DINAH. This is awful. We must demand an errata note.

TED. That's not bad though. Startling ability. You can't say fairer than that, love . . .

DINAH. They say you're dead.

TED. As a dramatist I am.

DINAH. And when this novel (*Indicating the typewriter.*) comes out – what are people going to say then?

TED (*reading*). Hang on! 'Though he lacked the grace and erudition of Miles Whittier –'

DINAH. Let me take it away and burn it –

TED (*holding her off*). 'Forrest's early death closed a career that promised more than there was time to fulfil.' Slimy bastard! In my entry. I'll bet I haven't slipped into *his* entry.

DINAH. Would you want to? Uergh!

TED. I shouldn't be alone, that's for sure.

DINAH. Not with all those crawlers who've been worming their way in all these years.

TED (*finding Whittier's entry*). Perhaps that accounts for the size of it. Look! 'Miles Whittier, born on a liner off the coast of Mozambique, 1947 –' How can you beat him? And even now he's less than forty.

DINAH. Ted, who told them you were dead?

TED. Who do you think? The form they sent happened to arrive the morning my last play closed. I *felt* dead.

DINAH. How did they think you returned the form? Two years after your death?

TED. Pretended to be my own executor. And with it sent an ironic assessment of my life's work. Funniest thing I'd done for years. How could I know they'd write it up so straight?

DINAH. Americans? You might have guessed.

TED. And died on April Fool's Day? I told them I'd been wasted away by a slow malignant tumour.

DINAH. Envy.

TED (*shakes his head*). Despair.

DINAH. No. Jealousy. It's killing you like unrequited lust. Your obsession with Miles' fame poisons all the parts I can't begin to reach. Caring for you, being your cook, secretary, washerwoman, call girl, protector, audience, mother to your kids, nursing you through all your terminal diseases –

TED. Nurse? That breaks my dream.

DINAH. All that means nothing beside the world's acclaim.

TED. I was dead, you were in your old nurse's uniform and you and he were – on my coffin.

He glares at the ottoman.

DINAH. You love him.

TED. What?

DINAH. Well, not him, his success. I've done all I can: coming to
this cultural desert, doing without papers and magazines,
censoring your mail, radio and TV, warning guests not to
mention Miles' name –

*He's sitting at the desk, head in hands, while she tries the heat of his
brow, and later takes his pulse.*

TED. Even so I hear it everywhere.

DINAH. Why don't you learn to count your blessings?

TED. I tried that. It takes so little time. Then I'm back to
counting *his*.

DINAH. Be positive. Start to work in an area where his fame
can't matter.

TED. The Antarctic?

DINAH. Finish your novel.

TED. Don't you mean 'start'?

DINAH (*looking at the page in the portable typewriter*). What?

TED. If you took a real interest in my work, you'd know that's
the page I wrote six months ago and have rewritten every day
since. I'm blocked and you didn't even notice.

DINAH. I must preserve myself and Becky and Tom. This isn't a
suicide pact.

TED. Why punish both of us by writing a novel nobody will
want? Anyway I'm not sure I can write that much prose.

DINAH. Try. That's what life is. Trying.

TED. Christ, isn't it?

DINAH. All right, die, but I'm not going with you. I'd sooner go
back to nursing patients who've still got the will to live.

TED. Even if I manage the book, who'll want it? Nobody wanted
my television series. Every single company turned it down.

DINAH. Except Mercia. They're about to accept it.

She makes to go but he holds her.

TED. Dinah, I do love you, not him.

DINAH. Then prove it.

He tries to embrace her, she accepts at first but he becomes passionate.

Not like that. That's not the kind of love I mean.

TED. You need a nice lie-down. On the ottoman.

DINAH (*evading him*). You do me a few nice pages then we'll see.

TED. You're right.

DINAH. Why start anything you can't finish. Till you've got your writing juices going again, it won't be any good. (*Aside.*) We've tried.

He turns to the desk, looks miserably at the page.

TED. That accounts for the title.

DINAH. What's that?

TED. 'Lead In His Pencil'.

DINAH. You mean being blocked is a kind of impotence?

TED. Right.

DINAH. Sounds a bit half-cock to me.

She goes, door 1.
    TED smiles, makes the first of many notes.

TED. Half-cock. Yes, I can use that.

Then he comes down to speak to the audience.

Now, if I were starting a play for the stage, that would be the exposition. Two people telling each other what each knows very well as a way of telling the audience.

He considers and shrugs.

You can start with a storm at sea or a tap dance or three witches – or a nightmare – to make the punters listen but sooner or later you have to catch up on the story so far.

He finishes his coffee.

How do you begin? How do you set the scene? In a play you can *see* the set but this is a novel. So – I'll have to describe

The Writer's Study. *All* his studies for the last twenty years. (*He shows a shotgun leaning against a wall.*) I keep it loaded ready for those pheasants. But what was it Chekhov said? 'A gun hanging on the wall in Act One must go off in Act Three'. (*He moves on the bookshelf.*) *Home Doctor*, *Who's Who*, Shakespeare, Bible and *Common Prayer*, *Rugby Songs*, Boswell's *Life of Johnson*, *The Story of O* . . .

As he shows this, an ominous tremolo is heard.
    He takes two books down, smacks them together; a cloud of dust.

His own plays, seldom acted. A few statuettes for writing the best comedies of some bygone years. Answering machine. One more defence against the outside world.

He switches on the outgoing message.

DINAH'S VOICE. Ted and Dinah Forrest are sorry they can't speak to you at the moment but –

He cuts it off. He moves to the upstage wall, shows door 1.

TED. Door. Sometimes leads to rest of house.

He opens it to show ACTOR ONE *as stage manager, checking a cue-light against a list on a clipboard. He's startled, dodges out of sight.* TED *sees, shuts the door quickly.*

And sometimes reveals our stage staff.

This should appear an accident and improvisation.
    He moves on to roll back one of the sliding doors of a cupboard. There may be three. Behind this one is a heap of junk of all kinds.

The lumber of his past that he carts from house to house. Always with him.

He slides back another door to show on a screen a life-size girlie photo. She's eating a peach and may move through a sequence of provocative poses.

A girlie calendar given him by his daughter Becky before she became a feminist.
April is the cruellest month, breeding
Lilacs out of the dead land,
Mixing memory and desire.

He closes the cupboard, moves to door 2.

Another door.

He opens it, revealing the WC. He fetches a bunch of cuttings from where they hang, like toilet-paper.

Cuttings from the days he dared to read the papers. 'We have grown used to Edward Forrest writing the best play of the year . . .'

ACTOR ONE *enters (door 2) as the* CRITIC, *and takes the paper cuttings.*

ACTOR ONE. He has now given us what we must all hope will be the worst.

TED. I should have flushed you down the khazi years ago.

ACTOR ONE *tears off the cutting and gives it to* TED. *He reads the next.*

ACTOR ONE. 'I fondly remember Forrest's first television plays, deadly accurate glimpses of the peacetime army such as *Blanco* and *You'd Find It If It Had Hairs Round It*, had a raw-boned quality sadly lacking from his first novel. This seems to have been cobbled together from scraps of an old television series. Even disguised as narrative, there is no mistaking the bland style, the jokes so fatuous they cry out for the Pavlovian stimulus of canned laughter.'

Canned laughter as the CRITIC *gives him this too and goes back to the lavatory.* TED *gives the laughter a look, turns to the ottoman.*

TED. A love seat, trunk or ottoman.

The weird tremolo is heard again as he opens the lid to show (anticlimax): it's full of papers.

Filing cabinet: his life's work in a box. Fifty plays, some letters to the Gas, some films they made and some they didn't. A television sitcom series they all turned down.

He takes out six scripts.

All except Mercia. Mercia just might come through. A new consortium bringing game shows and snooker to the border counties of Wales and England. The entire length of Offa's Dyke they can't wait to hear about the problems of a blocked playwright.

He moves to the desk, puts scripts upon it. He looks through binoculars at us.

And in the fourth wall the window, his only view of the world. Not always the same view, because this isn't always the same room. At this moment he looks out on an English country garden. Beyond the spacious lawn a copper beech and chestnut. Rough ground falls to a stream and sheep graze in a neighbour's meadow. They stare at him, he stares at them.

A fine spring day. One bit of scenery you wouldn't have to paint.

No. Of course Miles Whittier wouldn't even bother with all that. He'd get straight on. Be more straightforward. Straightforward, straight back.

He drops one of his scripts in the basket, sits to write.

Why not begin when Dinah and I were younger, before I'd given up hope? When the children were toddlers? Well, you couldn't in a play because you can't have toddlers acting on a stage, but this is a *novel* – so –

He puts a page in the machine; invents and types.

Their first flat had two rooms. Tom and Becky had cots in the Living Room. Ted wrote in the Bedroom, with a view across some derelict gardens to the back wall of a garment factory. He'd heard that somewhere London was swinging but not Kilburn. Kilburn was children.

He types. Sounds of screaming and fighting offstage. Lights change. He stops typing and pounds on his desk with his fists. He stands and goes to door 2, shouting:

For Chrissake, can't you keep the little bastards quiet for ten minutes?

He turns back to the desk as door 2 opens to admit ACTRESS TWO *and* ACTOR TWO *playing* BECKY *and* TOM, *their ages on their T-shirts: 3 and 1½. He's crying and she's chasing him. He wears an obviously full nappy.*

Now, now, who's being naughty?

BECKY. He is – Tom.

TED. Wrong. You are, Becky.

He tries to catch her, misses. She catches TOM, *smacks him.*

BECKY. Naughty boy. Naughty!

TOM falls down and lies on the floor, crying and kicking his legs.

TED. Now stop that. You're not to hit him.

BECKY. He's naughty.

TED picks up TOM, *flinches at his smell, holds him away.*

TED. He stinks to heaven, I know that.

BECKY. That's because he's done a bo-bo.

TED. An enormous one if I'm any judge.

BECKY. The biggest bo-bo in the world.

TED. But that's no reason to knock him down. And how many times have you been told not to come into Mummy and Daddy's bedroom when Daddy's trying to write his stories?

ACTRESS ONE comes in door 2 as DINAH, *carrying a small package.*

DINAH. I sent them in because it's time you were off. Your appointment's at ten.

TED. Meeting.

DINAH. What?

TED. Media people call it a meeting. Say 'Daddy's in a meeting' . . .

BECKY. 'Daddy's in a meeting'.

TOM kicks her from behind. She yells.

He pushed me.

DINAH. Serves you right for tormenting him.

BECKY. He's got to learn.

She smacks TOM, *who yells again.*

DINAH. Now that's enough.

She smacks BECKY, *who sobs. They continue thus.*

Did you get your work done?

TED. I got a few ideas down, yes, in case they won't cough up for the script I've already done.

DINAH. Why shouldn't they? They owe it to you.

TED (*putting the script in his briefcase*). In theory.

DINAH. They must. Don't you dare come home empty-handed!
We owe £300 already and next quarter's rent's due in
a fortnight –

TED. Yes, I know –

DINAH. – and I can't go on carrying these two up and down a
flight of 68 stairs –

TED. I know that, love, but could you let me have a pound
or two?

DINAH. What for?

TED. A bite of lunch.

DINAH. We can't afford it. Sandwiches.

She gives him the package, which he puts in his briefcase.

TED. There's the tube and I may have to buy a drink.

DINAH. Drink? Tell them how long it is since you bought *me* a
drink. Tell them what I'll be doing this morning.

TED. Yes, I know –

DINAH. Lugging these two with a bag of nappies down to the
launderette and later lugging them back again up 68 steps.
You tell them!

TED. Love, these are businessmen. They'll only give you money
if they're certain you don't need it. To him that hath it shall
be given.

DINAH. They need you too.

TED. Me? Alhambra Television need me?

DINAH. You writers. Without you they'd have no plays to go
between the adverts.

TED. They control the means of production. Read your Marx.
Read your Engels.

DINAH. When – now? Or at the launderette? Fat chance I've got
to read. Only what Billy Bull said to Minnie Moocow.

BECKY. Don't want that one. Want a new story.

TOM *moos and butts* BECKY. *They fight.*

TED. I'll see my agent too. She might have some money for us.

DINAH. Be back by three, that's all. I'm due at the Family Planning Clinic. We can't afford any more like these.

TED. No. I'll get off to business then. Kiss for Daddy?

He bends over TOM, *recoils from the smell.* TOM *kisses him.*

Christ!

DINAH. Don't get shit on your business shirt.

TED. No. Bye-bye.

He kisses BECKY *and* DINAH, *goes to door 1.*

DINAH. Come on, let Mummy clean him up.

She feels TOM's *bottom.*

TOM. Bo-bo.

DINAH. It's a *Guinness Book of Records* bo-bo, this one . . . isn't it, eh? Yes, it is.

They all go by door 2. TED *waves, watches.*

TED. With the spring of a gazelle, Ted ran from this fetid prison, so fleet of foot that he hardly touched the 68 steps between him and freedom. The freedom of the streets . . .

He throws open door 1. Blue sky with white clouds fills the opening. A psychedelic effect over the whole set. A burst of sixties music.

. . . where ready-looking girls flashed on Moulton bikes or folded their legs into mini-cars. London has discovered thighs!

He goes, closing the door.
The projection fades. The music ends. An awkward pause. ACTRESS TWO *comes back, door 2, half into her costume as a business girl.*

ACTRESS TWO (*to* TED, *who re-enters*). This costume change is still too fast.

TED *looks at the audience, goes to the wings.*

TED (*off*). She says that costume change is still too fast –

ACTRESS TWO. Perhaps I can take this chance to tell you why we're all playing several parts. The producer said, with so many theatres half-empty or going dark, any play with a cast larger than six would never recoup its capital. Equity said it was another attempt to reduce manning levels but in the end we agreed because we felt artistically we'd be *stretched*. We're not just here to fill theatres or feed the director's ego or help the author find out where his life went wrong, for Chrissake. We're here every night while they're off enjoying themselves –

TED has come back and waits, then gives her the line.

TED. Can I help you?

She stops, sulkily, sits at the desk and says in secretary voice:

ACTRESS TWO. Can I help you?

TED. Forrest to see Charles Upcraft.

The phone rings. She answers it.

ACTRESS TWO. Alhambra Television . . . which conference suite is that? . . . There are four all told . . . right . . .

She looks up at TED again.

TED. Edward Forrest to see –

ACTRESS TWO. Yes, just a minute, I'm on the phone. Hello? Sir shall be there. *Grazie, ciao.*

She puts down the phone. He starts again but she stops him with her hand, makes a note, then turns her face to him.

Now.

TED. Edward Forrest for Mister Upcraft.

ACTRESS TWO. Won't you take a seat? (*Then into the phone again.*) Mr. Forrest's here.

TED sits on the ottoman, takes up a magazine from the table, and speaks to us.

TED. Charles Upcraft was the executive producer of a successful television series called *Drifters*. His job was to keep the lowest paid workers in a state of grovelling obedience.

ACTRESS TWO. *Jawohl, danke.* (*She puts down the phone.*)

TED. The lowest paid being the writers – of course – and the small-part actors.

ACTOR TWO comes in, door 2, wearing a sou'wester, oilskins, boots, old salt's beard. ACTOR ONE follows as UPCRAFT, wearing heavy-rimmed glasses, shirtsleeves, rolled; speaks plummy public school updated with sixties slang.

ACTOR TWO. You didn't mind my popping in?

UPCRAFT. Any time, my old mate. What I'm here for.

ACTOR TWO. Just that my blessed agent thought the starring episodes you'd promised were a long time coming.

UPCRAFT. Trust me, episodes 34 to 40 will send you crashing through the fame barrier at a rate of knots. You'll be as well known in your local snug as your average – what d'you call those new stars, Jacqui?

ACTRESS TWO. Beatle?

UPCRAFT. Right. Your average Beatle.

ACTOR TWO. I'm much obleeged. Well, I must go down to the sea again in case they've got to my next wordless appearance. Cheers.

UPCRAFT (*after him*). Land is in sight.

ACTOR TWO goes by the wings. UPCRAFT welcomes TED.

My dear old mate, how's tricks? Come in.

He leads him towards door 2, turns.

Jacqui – Big White Chief him come darkest Acton –

TED. Kilburn.

UPCRAFT. Need heap big coffee like so. Otherwise powwow him bite dust mighty quick.

ACTRESS TWO (*all charm now*). Black or white?

TED. White, please. Four sugars.

She goes off at the side. UPCRAFT turns at the door, shuts it and moves towards the desk, steering TED back into the room that's now his office.

UPCRAFT. Come in, come in!

He clears the desk of scripts, dumping some in the basket, filing others in the cabinet, while TED *sits on a stool beside the desk.*

I kid you not, this goes down as Number One Horrendous Day of All Time. The absolute pits. Uninterrupted sunshine on the North Sea location when we need a force nine gale, trawlermen in and out of here all day deploring the size of their parts. But, he cried, let us turn without more ado to your script for *Drifters*. Believe me, matey, this I like. But *like*. I kid you not.

TED. Is it all right? As you know, I've never written for a series before.

UPCRAFT. Quintessential Forrest. Abrasive, acerbic, biliously antiromantic – trust me, it gets me where I live.

TED. That's a relief. After three drafts. Bloody glad to hear it fits the bill. We badly need the money.

UPCRAFT *does pantomime of looking about for a hidden voice.*

UPCRAFT. Fits the bill? Did I say that? Who said that? Hang about, old cock, I fear we've run into a tiny snag. A small snagette.

TED. Oh?

UPCRAFT. The first mate.

He mimes slitting his throat.

TED. But he's the only character with a breath of life.

UPCRAFT. Now steady as she goes –

TED. Suddenly amongst all those stereotyped Old Salts an awkward original rears his oilskins.

UPCRAFT. Avast, my hearty, he cried feebly. Man, this I like. The problem lies not in your writing. Truly.

TED. Where lies it then?

UPCRAFT. Yours is episode – um –

He consults the script on his desk.

TED. Twenty-three.

UPCRAFT. And – in 22, sad to say, the first mate is going to be swept overboard. In a high sea, if we can find one.

ACTRESS TWO *comes in with coffee.*

Ah, *danke, liebchen*, any bikkies?

ACTRESS TWO. Bikkies all gone soft.

UPCRAFT. Get bikkies!

He makes a gun with his fist, points at her, shoots. She mimes being wounded, struggles out, shuts the door. UPCRAFT sips coffee, makes appalled face.

Holy Mother of God.

He throws the contents of the cup over the front row of the audience. Some confetti falls out.

TED. You mean the first mate won't be in my episode at all?

UPCRAFT. Policy decision. You-know-who –

He points to the ceiling.

sent down a tablet from Sinai despatching him to Davy Jones's locker.

TED. Just like that? You didn't object?

UPCRAFT. Object? I did my tiny nut. The full Susan Hayward right there in the inner sanctum. Artistic integrity, I cried gamely, nationwide breakthrough, an upward leap in ratings, no alternative but to resign, the whole bit.

TED. And?

UPCRAFT. We reached a compromise. Yahweh persuaded me not to resign and I agreed to drown the first mate.

TED. Wonderful.

UPCRAFT. It's out of our hands, Ted, love. The actor who plays the mate has been caught in a cottage. Up to no good.

TED. Well, as long as it was in the privacy of his own home.

UPCRAFT (*incredulous*). I said a cottage.

TED (*shrugs*). All these actors can afford country homes.

UPCRAFT. A cottage is a public gents'. Where have you been, matey?

TED. Tied to the desk doing episode 23.

ACTRESS TWO returns with a plate.

ACTRESS TWO. Bikkies from next door, crisp as a virgin's knickers.

UPCRAFT. How would *you* know?

ACTRESS TWO. Charming. That really is your actual charming.

He takes the plate, she goes. He offers.

UPCRAFT. No, you may be the best scripter in the land, I an ace producer but just try telling that to Our Father Which Is In The Penthouse Suite.

He points upwards, gives TED *the script.*

Give all the mate's big scenes to the bosun and let me have that soonest.

TED. Before I do it the fourth time, you'll give me the cheque?

UPCRAFT. Which cheque is that, love?

TED. For the final draft.

UPCRAFT. *Acceptance* of the final draft.

TED. Accept it then. You say you like it –

UPCRAFT. But *like* –

He tries to steer TED *towards the door.* TED *puts the script in his brief-case.*

TED. And I can't be blamed for the man overboard.

UPCRAFT. You're not blaming me?

TED. No I suppose it's an act of God.

He points upwards, UPCRAFT *laughs.*

UPCRAFT. Amen! But I can't authorise payment till the mate's gone down.

TED. So it's stale*mate*.

UPCRAFT (*laughs again*). Hah! How's the family?

TED. Oh, they're fine –

UPCRAFT. And the delectable Susie?

TED. *Dinah*'s not too bad, though it isn't easy coping with two toddlers in a third floor flat up 68 stairs.

UPCRAFT *moves him up to door 2.*

She was hoping we'd pay off our rent arrears with your cheque and put down the deposit –

UPCRAFT *continues out by the door, shuts it firmly behind* TED *who hears it shut and stands alone.*
   Pause.

– on a second-hand van so we wouldn't have to lug them everywhere on the bus.

He comes down.

Out again among London's thighs. The breasts. The jutting little rumps. In his voyeur's raincoat, Ted entered the Royal Parks which were by this time a choppy sea of fornication. Couples queued for a patch of royal grass. Come in, 58, your time is up. On he stumbled up the back passages of Soho, averting his eyes from strip-clubs and their limp members till at last he climbed to the office of his agent Nancy Fraser.

He sits on the stool beside the desk again. ACTRESS ONE *comes through door 1, wearing a silk scarf, and glasses on a string around her neck.* NANCY *is a volatile middle-aged woman. She speaks in an almost unbroken monologue.*

NANCY (*shouting off*). So you mean we haven't any dough at all for Ted?

Someone answers off. NANCY *interrupts.*

What about the New Zealand rights of *Don't Mess Me About, Chiefey*!?

She listens to the answer, slams the door, comes to sit at the desk.

He says you've already had that.

TED. Yes. Thirteen pounds, ten shillings.

NANCY. That was a help surely?

TED. Don't think I'm complaining, Nancy. It's when the bills start coming in and you've nothing in the bank to –

NANCY. Don't tell me I didn't warn you, though, when you left that ghastly teaching job –

TED (*unheard while she goes on*). I was a compositor in a print room –

NANCY. – you'd only be swapping the teaching treadmill for the television chain-gang. But you're all the same, you writers. Your friend Ragtag –

TED. Bobtail.

NANCY. – rang the other day from his hovel in Huddersfield –

TED. In Cardiff –

NANCY. And all the time he was droning on I could hear this baby screaming and his poor wife going demented and I felt guilty that I'd ever encouraged him to leave his printing job.

TED. Teaching job –

NANCY. So I had to do something to help.

She goes to door 1, shouts off.

Gary, did you tell Bob Tail we'd sold his play to Germany?

As GARY *answers, she shuts the door, comes back.*

And now look at you with this awful Skippers or Kippers or whatever-it-is waiting for Domesday for the dough and when it comes it's peanuts.

The phone rings. She at once picks it up and holds it near her mouth while she finishes.

If you're going to be a whore at least before you open your legs make sure you're properly paid. Hullo?

She laughs. While she talks, she goes on working, signing contracts, throwing out scripts, etc.

Charlie, darling! I wasn't talking *to* you or *about* you. Are you brown? . . . I'll bet . . . even *that's* brown?

She laughs, spins on the chair. TED *takes from his brief-case the package of sandwiches and eats.*

Now honestly, it wasn't too bad a place to get paid a fortune for *not* writing a film . . . right, dear, fire away.

TED *raises a chair above her head.* CRITIC *comes on, door 2.*

ACTOR ONE (*as* CRITIC). The scene where he batters his agent to death in her office aims to be Absurdist but manages to be merely absurd.

TED. Think so?

ACTOR ONE. Yes.

TED takes down the chair. The CRITIC *goes.* TED *munches his lunch.*

NANCY (*who hasn't stopped*). I've told them you are a writer of the highest integrity and anything less than twenty-five thousand smackeroos would be quite unethical. So the ball's in their court. Bye-ee. (*She puts down the phone.*) Poor Charlie Rubens, darling, going through HELL. The Rubenses have got an entourage of parasites stretching from their oast house in Kent to their castle in Tuscany, all stealing Charlie's dough and mainlining on heroin and there's poor Charlie in the midst of this maelstrom trying to finish *Middlemarch* and going slowly demented. His children come to him and say 'Daddy, we're all limited companies but it hasn't made us happy', and he says 'I'll buy you a cheetah' and they burst into tears and he says, 'One each – I meant one each'.

TED. Awful. Well our main problem is next month's rent, so if you –

NANCY *clears* TED's *bag of sandwiches, drops it into the litter bin. She makes for door 1, opens it, calls.*

NANCY. We did send that letter off to Columbia Pictures about Charlie Rubens. Miles darling, *do* come in. Why are you skulking about out here?

She drags in ACTOR TWO, *very casual and elegant, polite, humble. We hear 'Long Live the King, May He Live Forever' from Handel's Zadok the Priest. All hold their positions,* TED *trying to retrieve his lunch.*

TED. How could I have failed to hear that leitmotif at the time?

MILES. Gary said you had someone with you.

NANCY. No, darling. Only Ted. D'you know each other? Ted Forrest – this is one of my new boys, Miles Whittier. Just down from Oxford –

MILES. Cambridge actually. Marvellous to meet you.

TED rises, they shake hands.

NANCY. He's sent me a wonderful TV play. Tremendously exciting.

MILES. I'm one of your greatest fans. *Don't Mess Me About, Chiefey* – one of the best television plays of the last ten years.

TED. Thank you, thank you.

MILES. You always know the real thing when you see it, don't you agree? And then you feel elation that anyone could be that good and despair that you yourself never will.

NANCY. Yes, but we can't *sell* him. His stage plays anyway. I've just been telling him why. Your poor old tired businessman who is the staple audience doesn't want an evening class, he wants an evening *out*. Not endless scenes of family life or long-forgotten battles. Yawn, yawn, yawn, darling. There's not enough *vice* in you. D'you remember when you nearly got a film and they wanted you in Paris to talk about it and you tried to borrow the dough to take Alice as well?

TED. Dinah.

NANCY. I said, 'You're not taking your wife to *Paris*? Like taking a ham sandwich to a banquet.' D'you remember?

TED. Yes.

NANCY. And it's caught on because I hardly ever call her Dinah now, do I?

TED (*unheard*). No. Usually Alice.

NANCY. It's always simply The Ham.

MILES. I feel I already know her – from your plays. That high fidelity is one of your great strengths.

NANCY. Ah, this cheque's for you, darling, the advance on your play, save us the stamp, there's a dear.

TED *hopes but she gives the cheque to* MILES.

TED (*to us*). *He's* the one I should have battered to death. If only people wore their futures in their faces – or around their heads as in the old paintings. Haloes or unearthly glows.

NANCY. No Ted, you must learn to spread your wings. Sign on with a tramp steamer. Smuggle arms to terrorists. Forget the kitchen sink, forget the poor old Ham. At the very least have an affair, find an obliging little tart, darling.

TED (*to* MILES *while she talks*). Come on, I'll buy you a drink.

TED *leads* MILES *towards door 2.*

NANCY. And don't mention your trollop to poor old Alice.

TED. Wouldn't think of it.

NANCY goes, door 1. She reopens the door almost at once and shouts to TED.

NANCY. Or is it Dinah?

She slams the door again. TED *moves to the shelves, left, where drinks have been served from a hatch. The sounds of a pub.*

TED. I felt sorry for him, protective. He was so young, so hopeful. He had such a high opinion of me, though how he knew my play was the best for ten years was a mystery as he couldn't have been much more than 14. I must be getting on, thought Ted, when even the playwrights start looking young. (TED *takes him his beer and Scotch.*)

MILES. What's this?

TED. Beer with a whisky chaser. Beer's where we came from, whisky's where we're going. To the top.

MILES. To the top.

They drink.

When we're the whisky people, we'll be the new oligarchy. Artists never rule anything. They sing a few songs, that's all.

TED. We sway their minds.

MILES. Do we? Ninety-five years of Bernard Shaw and we've still got vivisection. Seventy years of Kipling and where's the Empire? Orwell told us that Britain would become airstrip one and did we stop it? No. Art never expresses anything but itself.

TED (*knowing it*). Oscar Wilde.

MILES. He who rides a hobby horse tends to come a cropper.

TED (*unsure*). Dr Johnson?

MILES (*modest shake of the head*). Me. Any writer who deals in proper-gander must be a proper goose. Me again.

TED. Yes, on the other hand 'Thou shalt not read the Bible for its prose style.'

MILES. Wystan Auden.

TED. Yes.

MILES. When my first play went on at university, some
undergraduate critic asked me what it was going on about.
I said about 7.30 with a 3 o'clock matinee. Same again?
(*He makes off for more drinks.*)

TED. Whisky oiled our tongues. The more we drank, the more
cultured pearls we cast around the public bar. Simply couldn't
face Dinah without.

ACTRESS ONE *comes back as* DINAH. TED *moves into the set,
taking off his raincoat, throwing his briefcase onto the desk.*

DINAH. Nothing, did you say?

TED. Nothing. They only pay on acceptance.

DINAH (*tensely*). What if they never accept?

TED. They never pay.

DINAH. You give everything and they give nothing?

TED. It's called Capital-and-Labour.

DINAH. Oh, thanks for telling me. I still haven't had time to get
started on Marx or Engels since you left this morning.
Too busy lugging the kids down 68 steps and – later lugging
them back up again –

TED. What do'you think *I've* been doing?

DINAH. Drinking beer by the smell of your breath.

TED. I had a beer, yes. With a charming boy called Whittier.
Nancy thinks he's Aeschylus so the odds are he won't go far.

ACTRESS TWO *enters with a toy elephant. She's* BECKY *again.*

DINAH. Give me back the pound. I'm late for the clinic.

BECKY. Don't talk too loud. Babar's going bye-byes.

TED *shows* DINAH *the coins from his pocket.*

DINAH. What's this?

TED. What's left.

DINAH. You spent all we had on beer while I was lugging them
up and down 68 –

TED (*cracking*). Not all, no. Some was on whisky.

DINAH. You drank whisky?

BECKY (*to her*). Naughty Mummy. Hush!

DINAH (*to her*). Don't dare speak to me like that.

TED. It's casting bread on water.

DINAH. What?

TED. In the fullness of time it will come back.

DINAH. Not with us it won't. It'll go soggy and sink.

TED has put paper in the machine and is typing.

What are you doing?

TED. Some ideas for a scene.

She rips the paper out, crumples it, throws it into his face.

DINAH. You self-centred bastard.

TED. Belt up, woman, before I make you.

He threatens to hit her. BECKY *hits him from behind.*

BECKY. No. Becky hit you. Babar hit you.

He turns and strikes her. She falls, crying.

TED. And Babar can go out of the window and into the yard –
the elephants' graveyard.

He grabs the elephant and throws it into audience.

BECKY. Don't like Daddy.

DINAH (*hugging her*). He's had too much to drink. It makes
him funny.

BECKY. Not funny. Nasty.

DINAH *cries too.*

TED. Shut up, both of you. Tomorrow I'll get a job in the Print
again. I'm still in the union. I'll work all week and write at
night, like I used to, all right? It's not the end of the world,
eh? We've got each other.

He approaches to hug them but they cry louder.

It's not as though we're hungry.

BECKY. Babar's hungry.

TED. Then give him a fucking biscuit!

Noise at highest level. The phone rings. TED *answers, lifting the receiver of the desk telephone.*

Hullo? . . . Nancy? No, no worse than any other time . . . only you'll have to speak up.

He turns on DINAH *and* BECKY, *threatens violence again. They cry and he holds the receiver towards them, lets* NANCY *hear.*

Sorry? . . . Well, two toddlers in a two-roomed flat, it's hardly surprising, is it?

DINAH. Come on, Becky, let's ask these nice mummies and daddies if they'll throw back Babar.

TED (*one hand over ear*). Of course I've heard of them. I wrote a play about them once, d'you perhaps remember? About the Peasants' Revolt? Revolting peasants were out that year so no one bought it.

DINAH (*over this*). I'll put Tom into his pushchair and you're both coming with me to the family planning. It isn't safe to leave you here with – (*She shouts at* TED.) – a drunken thug! (*They go off.*)

DINAH *and* BECKY *go down to the audience and recover the elephant.* BECKY *goes out with it.*

TED (*still into the phone*). Yes, I know what *ciné vérité* means. Faking plays to look real. He's one of those, yes, and – yes – grand what? No, don't try for more. That's more than enough . . . any time, I can meet them any time . . .

DINAH (*returning, to him, loud*). In case you didn't hear me, I'm taking the kids with me to the clinic. They're not safe here with a dipso-maniac.

He grabs her by the arm. She struggles.

TED. Yes. Goodbye, Nancy.

He puts down the phone.

DINAH. Leave me alone.

TED. No, listen, love. I'm up for a film. If we get it we'll be rich.

DINAH (*faltering*). What?

TED. Jack Straw and the Rebels.

DINAH. That's marvellous. You've already done the research for that Peasants' Revolt play nobody would buy – all about Wat Tyler –

TED. No, love, listen. Jack Straw's a pop star. His group is called The Rebels. That's the money we shall earn if I get it.

He shows her a figure written down.

DINAH. Four pounds?

TED. Look at the noughts.

DINAH. Four thousand?

TED. Or – as we call it in the movie business – four grand. She says I must do it for Alice's sake.

DINAH. Alice who?

TED. I think she means you.

The phone rings. He answers.

Hullo? . . . well, I guessed that –

He puts down the phone.

Yes, she does.

DINAH. Oh, Ted, d'you think you'll get this job? It would solve all our problems.

TED. No, we shan't. We must not pin our hopes. Like winning the pools, that's the sort of thing that happens to someone else. Not us.

DINAH. I know. But we can keep our fingers crossed.

TED. We shan't get it. Understand?

She nods, kisses him and goes. TED *turns to us.*

But we did. Well, it was the sixties and all of us lived in those days by writing propaganda for Swinging Britain. A barefaced American lie, of course, but people longed to believe it. Standing here in the Aching Eighties, I can see why. Staring out the window of my eighteenth-century manor from behind Laura Ashley curtains in a wild-flower pattern of Thatcherite nostalgia . . . well, it's hard to remember how up-to-date everything used to be. So we did the film. And it changed our lives. With the money I wrote the stage play I'd promised Dinah.

From door 2 comes ACTOR ONE *as the* CRITIC.

ACTOR ONE. The name of Edward Forrest is new to me yet how skilfully this novice can command the stops to an utterance of harmony!

TED. I am ashamed to say I can still recite some of these by heart.

ACTOR ONE. Though his attempts to hide the mundane naturalism of the early scenes with tricks and gimmicks put me in mind of the dreary solipsisms of Pirandello.

TED (*going to him*). I'm not hiding anything. It's the well-made play that's all devices. You're used to the well-made play.

ACTOR ONE. These days? Fat chance.

He goes into the wings as TED *continues to us.*

TED. The novelty of marriage had worn off long ago and Edward took to reading pornography while Dinah coped with the home. Now he was a minor celebrity journalists came to his new house to interview him. What had only been a fantasy now stepped into his room.

He opens the door of the cupboard. ACTRESS TWO *is now* APRIL, *dressed in rainwear, etc., with a tape recorder and notebook. She speaks American.*

She was from *Vogue* or *Look* or *Life or Death* . . .

She steps into the room and puts her recorder on his desk.

APRIL. OK. Lemme get this started.

TED. Thou art thy mother's glass and she in thee
Calls back the lovely April of her prime.

APRIL. That's fine. So – (*Checking among her cuttings and notes.*) – about Jack Straw and The Rebels. You said, quote, they were no threat to established order unquote.

TED. Somewhere to the right of Prince Philip.

APRIL. I like it. The director moved to Hollywood and you to Chiswick?

She pronounces the 'w'.

TED. Chissick, yes.

APRIL (*takes up the binoculars and looks over the audience*). A Victorian row house with a strip of yard that's a lookalike for the yards either side. Two toddlers tormenting a tabby-cat in a sandbox. Your wife weeding the flowerbeds. A capable mother. Runs a tight ship, I imagine?

TED. Dinah's the real creator. You should be talking to *her*. Grows food and flowers, plants mulberries and walnuts, trees so slow we'll never taste their fruit. Breeds babies, cares for cats, smiles at strangers, she's all Faith In Future, an unknown artist. I'm only an entertainer. Talk to her.

APRIL (*still with glasses, not hearing*). Who's the hippy?

TED. He's her mother's help.

APRIL. I'm surprised she needs any.

TED. It goes with the mortgage, the Moffat hob, the Moulton bikes . . .

APRIL. We met at the door when he let me in. Stoned out of his skull.

TED. Oh, he's off the hard stuff now. When he first came, his wrists were like a pin-cushion.

APRIL. Where did he come from?

TED. Answered an advert in *The Lady*. When I saw him I wasn't keen but he appealed to the nurse in Dinah –

APRIL. She likes helping lame ducks? It's in character.

TED. Well, she married *me*.

APRIL (*turns to him as he sits at the desk*). You telling me she saw you as a lame duck?

TED. Perhaps I was.

APRIL. Well, now she'd better get used to the fact you're running with the ball.

TED. I'm what?

APRIL. A new star. You had a London hit and now a smash
on Broadway. Surely to God you know about the aphrodisiac
of fame?

*She unbuttons her denim tunic, takes it off. She's wearing a blouse or
shirt, and begins undoing that too.* TED's *alarmed, stands.*

TED. Is it too warm in here?

APRIL. It's like a sauna. Don't you feel it?

TED. Shall I open the door?

He goes towards it.

APRIL. Lock the door. Open the window.

He obeys.

TED. I keep it shut to stop the noise but if you're uncomfortable –

*He mimes opening the casement. Sounds of London traffic, aircraft, dogs,
etc., come in.*

APRIL. The reviews in London were terrific, am I right?

ACTOR ONE *comes from door 2.*

(*Undoing her skirt.*) But in New York they were even better.

ACTOR ONE. (*American*) Another British play has come to
gladden the moribund Broadway season, a Proustian Look
Back in Languor replete with stoical one-liners and life-
enhancing love.

APRIL *goes on undressing.* TED *takes off his glasses, wrist-watch
and shoes.*

Your reviewer too was replete after supper in the Polynesian
eatery on the same block, where Gauguin girls place leis
around your neck as soon as the captain bids you aloha.

APRIL, *now in lingerie, lies on the desk, aided by* ACTOR ONE.

APRIL. Have you any idea what power it gives a person to be
praised like that? To be rich is good, to be famous, to be up
there receiving awards, that's a sexual charge in a million.
Why d'you think there's so much kissing, so much embracing
and caressing when they hand out those bronze phalluses?

TED *sprays her body with water.*

Jesus, is that good!

TED puts down the spray and begins fumbling with his trousers. APRIL groans with pleasure.

ACTOR ONE. The first hint of his oxymoron quality is in the scene of his seduction by the brazen and delectable April. When she asks:

APRIL. You want me to help with that?

She and he fumble together.

ACTOR ONE. We feel the action lurch towards erotic farce.

TED. The fastener's caught.

ACTOR ONE. One feels a certain sympathy for the able young actress whose task it is to flesh out this hackneyed male fantasy –

TED. But flesh it out she does, with no holds barred.

ACTOR ONE. Forrest employs this deft device –

TED. Shut up and get off!

He pushes him towards door 2, slams it on him as he goes. As he turns back:

Breeding lilacs out of the dead land . . .

APRIL. Mixing memory and desire –

The door's tried. TED freezes.

TED. Ssh!

There's a gentle knock.

Just a minute!

He goes to the tape machine, switches on typing.

Must finish this speech.

He runs back to put on his glasses, shoes, watch. APRIL collects her clothes. He talks as though he's considering his work.

Um – let me see now – yes, that's good – why don't you climb in here?

He pushes APRIL towards the ottoman.

APRIL. You wanna put me in a closed box? I'd feel dead.

TED. Shush. She'll hear you.

She makes for door 2, opens it. ACTOR ONE *reaches for her.*

ACTOR ONE. Behind every door lurk the ghosts of Pinero, Ben Travers, Brian Rix.

He moves her to the cupboard and off among a row of hanging clothes. Vapour escapes. TED *turns off the typing tape, goes to door 1, opens it to admit* ACTOR TWO *as* SPEED, *the mother's help, a long-haired sixties hippie with a dopey manner, who stands spellbound by the coffee cup in his hand.*

TED. I thought it was Dinah.

SPEED. No, it's really not. I'm Speed. The mother's help. Remember?

TED. I mean I thought it was Dinah before I saw you – never mind.

SPEED. And your wife said I could help by bringing you this – um –

He stares at it, trying to identify it.

TED. Cup of coffee, yes, thanks.

He takes it and shuts the door on him. TED *comes down, puts the cup on the desk, as* ACTOR ONE *comes from door 1.*

ACTOR ONE. And so we welcome a new playwright whose way of making us belly-laugh one moment and cry the next might well be called Funny Boo-Hoo.

TED. Oh, do leave off. I should have burnt you all years ago.

ACTOR ONE. But you didn't, did you? And in your darkest moments we have the power to remind you that you were once among the stars.

He goes.

TED. Never reply to a critic, it's feeding the hand that bites you. April turned to May. Or more properly Mai, a Swedish student who was doing my plays as part of her English degree at Uppsala University. She later sent me a recorded account of her visit.

He switches on the tape machine left by APRIL. *Eerie music.*

MAI (*voice*). Both my tutor and I were surprised when Mr Forrest agreed to answer my questions and invited me to his charming Georgian house in a London suburb called Highgate. Although I had thoroughly prepared myself, I was naturally rather anxious and –

TED *has fetched* The Story of O *from the shelf and now switches off the machine. He takes over.*

TED. 'Approaching the house, I was consumed by a sudden fear that made it well-nigh impossible to breathe, my rather full breasts rose and fell, so fearful was I of whatever fate awaited me. I found him at the door of his study, no longer young but far better-looking than his photograph had led me to expect. He had the arrogant assurance of an English milord. I was required to wash away all trace of the outside world and as I emerged he stood appraising me as though I were some china figurine.'

He has opened door 2 which has a glass panel. ACTRESS TWO *emerges, as* MAI *through a cloud of steam, wearing only a towel. She's blonde after being dark as* APRIL.

TED. Come.

MAI. He commanded and I knew instantly that any dawdling or defiance would be swiftly punished.

TED. Let your arms hang at your sides.

He sits her on a stool.

MAI. Still damp from my bath, my pulse racing, my lips moist and half-open, I awaited his fancy.

ACTOR ONE *enters wearing a black hood and carrying a glass of brandy and a riding crop. He bows to* TED, *gives him the glass. He finds that* MAI *has brought up her hands protectively. He gives a quick switch of the crop and she brings them down. Before he goes,* ACTOR ONE *turns to us.*

ACTOR ONE. *The Story of O*, redone by Feydeau.

He goes. MAI *looks intently towards the audience.*

MAI. One wall was a huge mirror. In vain I averted my gaze but some compulsion drew me back and there, as well as my own defenceless image, were faint specks of red light. At once I knew them for the glowing ends of cigars. Beyond that glass sat rows of watching men. And, for all I knew, women too.

TED. Armagnac?

He holds the goblet to her lips and allows her to sip.

His steady gaze seemed to probe her inmost being –

MAI. But, emboldened by the coursing spirit, I risked his displeasure by asking the first question I had prepared before starting this fateful voyage: How highly do you rate the comedies of Alan Ayckbourn?

TED recoils and draws himself up.

Only by a sharp intake of breath did he betray his anger.

He swallows the brandy in one gulp.

Seeing him recoil, I demanded: Do the plays of Arnold Wesker advance or retard the advent of Socialism?

TED rounds on her with an angry snarl. She is up now and moving towards him.

Are sadism and violence vital elements in the success of Harold Pinter?

He retreats and she presses forward to the shelves, where he cowers like Dracula before the garlic.

What will be the effect of the new feminist drama on male pornography?

With a cry, he threatens to throw a chair at her. There's a knock on the door. He signals MAI to be quiet.

TED. Hello? Who is it?

DINAH (*off*). Me. Why's the door locked?

TED. I'm listening to this piece.

DINAH (*off*). What piece?

TED. From Sweden. She came to see me one day when you were out and later sent me her piece.

MAI. Do you see your plays as advocating revolution like those of David Mercer, Edward Bond, Trevor Griffiths, David Edgar, John McGrath, John Arden, Margaretta D'Arcy – ?

DINAH. Turn her off and let me in.

MAI. Willy Russell, Caryl Churchill, Howard Barker –

TED. Hang on.

MAI. David Hare, Howard Brenton –

TED has dragged her to the cupboard and opens it to show ACTOR ONE *entering through the clothes.*

ACTOR ONE. It is as though Strindberg had written a bedroom farce.

TED shuts the door.

MAI. – or do you see them as supporting the status quo like those of Alan Bennett, John Osborne, Robert Bolt, Michael Frayn, Julian Mitchell, Tom Stoppard, Christopher Hampton.

Meanwhile MAI *has escaped to door 2, opens it to show* ACTOR TWO *without trousers.*

ACTOR ONE. Your best bet for a real hoot. Gor blimey, strewth and loveaduck.

She slams it. TED *opens the ottoman lid. Steam escapes from both.*

MAI. John Mortimer, Simon Gray, Peter Shaffer –

DINAH (*knocking*). Ted, will you let me in? It's important.

TED. Coming, coming!

MAI. Charles Wood, Peter Nichols and Bob Tail?

Having got her in and shut the lid, TED *returns to the recorder and turns it off. Then he unlocks the door, runs back and sits on the ottoman, taking the recorder with him.* DINAH *comes in.*

DINAH. I thought you were working, not drooling over some Nordic piece.

TED. Doesn't this sound like work to you?

He switches on again.

MAI (*voice*). And how does the work of North Country playwrights like Peter Terson, E.A. Whitehead, Willis Hall, Henry Livings, Alan Bleasdale – ?

DINAH. Turn it off and get out of my way.

TED. What d'you want?

He stands, turning off the tape.

DINAH. Some tax returns from years ago. They're in the ottoman.

TED. The ottoman? How many have we got of 'em?

DINAH. An awful lot of 'em. We should get shot of 'em.

TED. Give them to the totter-man.

Recorded laughter. DINAH *gets there first and opens to find only papers.*

That ottoman hasn't got a bottom on.

TED *considers, sits at the desk and begins typing.* DINAH *looks about. Some vapour hovers in the room.*

DINAH. You haven't taken up smoking again?

TED. No. It's steam. Dry ice. Solid carbon dioxide. It always goes with a memory. A flashback or a fantasy.

DINAH. I must say it's all right for some. Being paid to wallow in daydreams, not having to concern themselves with income tax, insurance, children's trust or pension fund. After all these years being poor, you think it's wonderful to have earned all this money from –

Reading off invoices.

Berlin, Brussels, Santiago, Tel Aviv – but someone has to worry or before we know where we are we'll owe more tax than we've saved and then we shan't know where we are.

TED *watches her, spreading files on the floor, sorting them. He crosses to her, crouches beside her.*

TED. Dinah, my dear, don't separate yourself. We've shared the rough times, so why should the smooth ones only be mine?

DINAH. Go and stick your head in a fantasy. I'll do the worrying about what happens if your next play fails.

TED. Even if it does, we're wealthier than we've ever been. Your pessimism is a fantasy too. I'm running with the ball.

DINAH (*disgusted*). What?

TED. I didn't say it. That journalist, April.

DINAH. And she seemed so nice.

TED. Such perfect teeth.

DINAH. Oh, lovely. Is that what Americans mean by putting their money where their mouth is?

She finds the papers, puts the others in the ottoman and shuts it.

TED. We promised for better, for worse. This is the better, love, don't miss it.

DINAH. Well?

ACTOR TWO *as* SPEED *appears at door 2.*

SPEED. That young bloke's arrived.

DINAH. Already? Christ, where's the morning gone?

TED. Who is it?

DINAH. You invited your friend to lunch. What's his name – Miles something –

TED. *Our* friend. As much your friend as mine.

DINAH. Where is he?

SPEED. In the Lounge.

DINAH. The Living-room.

SPEED (*feigning amazement*). Right . . . really fantastic, man. 'Living-room!' Wow!

DINAH. Did you offer him a drink?

SPEED *shakes his head, makes to go, stops when she goes on.*

When a guest arrives, you must offer him a sherry. Some time I'll show you which glasses go with which. All right?

SPEED. Like . . . I didn't come as a butler . . . you know?

DINAH. Speed, I haven't the time for a demarcation dispute.

SPEED. Came as a mother's help.

DINAH. Yes and it would help this mother very much if you learnt to entertain our guests. And very likely help you too to be less shy and put down by life if you acquired a few social graces. Making them feel at ease you'd be more easy in yourself.

SPEED *stands, looking away from her.*

Speed? Believe me?

He looks up, nods. She smiles. He goes. She pauses in the doorway.

Come and talk to Miles while I finish lunch but don't tell him you've sold the film rights –

TED. He knows already.

DINAH. – or at any rate that you're getting the best play of the year award. Ask about *him*. He needs to be bucked up.

She goes. TED *makes a note on the desk pad.*

TED. Lame ducks. We were all lame ducks to her. Even Miles. That was her vocation and reward. She had no films to write, no awards to receive with a deprecating speech. She had only Becky, who was now at primary school, and Tom at the Montessori and Speed, her mother's help. Help!

Lights change so that night is suggested by pools on door 2 and the ottoman. TED *goes to one side. Calls, as though drowning:*

Help!

ACTOR ONE *comes on late from the wings with a jacket and suitcase. He helps* TED *on with the jacket.*

ACTOR ONE. One can't help feeling that an actor as accomplished as (*Insert actor's name.*) is wasted in the part of the Critic, a piece of petty author's vengeance if ever there was one.

He goes.

TED (*calling*). Dinah!

He moves into the room, now in night light. DINAH *comes, door 2, in a nightdress, cleaning her teeth.*

DINAH. You said you were staying away till morning.

TED. I was lonely for you.

DINAH. After one day?

TED. What's so strange? Would you rather I'd got some chick in Manchester? Some dolly-bird? Some piece.

He goes to her, kisses her; she averts her face.

DINAH. I'm cleaning my teeth.

TED (*tastes*). Spearmint . . . Nice. (*Taking off his jacket, going to the cupboard.*) They got through the recording early and the last train from Manchester –

He slides back the cupboard door to hang the jacket. It's a wardrobe with his suits on a bar. Standing among them is the naked SPEED. *Canned laughter.* TED *takes it in.*

DINAH. Why don't you put his gown on?

SPEED *takes it from a hook behind the door, puts it on. Now he's less dopey, almost normal.*

SPEED. I didn't dare move. Only just had time to dodge in there when I heard him coming.

DINAH (*to* TED). I meant to tell you. I was going to sooner or later.

SPEED. Better this way. Straight to the point.

DINAH. Didn't you even guess?

TED. Are you saying this isn't the first time?

DINAH (*to* SPEED). He didn't guess.

SPEED. You don't need her any more, man . . .

TED. Where d'you get off telling me what I need?

DINAH. You haven't for ages. Any of us. You don't even see us. Your eyes glaze over the moment the children start to tell about their projects or nativity plays –

SPEED. Or *Magic Roundabout* or *Bill and Ben* –

TED. I listen to every word.

DINAH. You hear them out. Then talk about yourself.

TED. I'm not very concerned about *Blue Peter*'s tortoise, no, or what Andy Pandy said to Itchky-koo or whatever she's called . . .

SPEED. Loobie Loo.

DINAH. It's my world. I don't belong in *yours*. I'm not an actress, I'm a nurse.

SPEED. Dinah's got so much to give, man, and all she wants is someone to give it *to*.

DINAH. While you were struggling, needing help, I had a place in your life. But what can I do now everybody wants you – all those journalists, those student groupies?

SPEED. When you first met Plum, you needed her. And she cured you like she's curing me.

TED. *I* wasn't a junkie! *I* had a broken ankle.

DINAH. Why don't we talk about this in the morning? We're going to wake the children –

TED. Don't you think it's time they were told?

DINAH. They know already. (*She imitates a child.*) Speed's kissing Mummy.

TED *hangs his jacket in the wardrobe, closes the doors.*

TED. Then if we wake them they can join us.

SPEED (*as ACTOR TWO*). No they can't.

TED. I can't see the harm now, can you?

SPEED. Well, Tom can't anyway.

TED. Why not?

ACTOR TWO. Because – (*Makes signs to say he plays* TOM *too.*)

TED. Oh sorry. (*He makes a note on the desk pad, crossing out an idea.*)

SPEED. OK, right, I was on speed and shooting up and sniffing coke, right? Freaking out because my dad was a regimental sergeant-major. And Plum just took my hand and told me I could stop fighting. It was all over. And now I only smoke the occasional joint.

DINAH (*takes his hand*). More in a spirit of nostalgia than anything.

SPEED. Right.

TED. Then, of course, if he kicked the stuff entirely you'd have nothing to cure him of.

SPEED. Jesus, man, grass isn't even a habit. You know nothing. Where've you *been*?

DINAH (*gently*). Nigel, please.

TED (*to us*). That *was* his name.

SPEED. I'm sorry, Plum. Lost my cool.

TED. And Plum was *his* name for *her*. (*To* DINAH:) Is it because you're sweet and round and tasty? Or soft to bite into? Full of juice?

She squeezes SPEED*'s hand.* TED *goes to a dictionary on the bookshelf and looks up a word.*

DINAH. Please, Ted, let's try not to hurt one another. Leave me with someone who wants me, who can use what little I have to give. I'll sleep in the children's room tonight. You can stay here in ours.

TED (*reading*). Plum. Plum–tree. The female pudenda, Shakespeare. Compare plum–tree shaker, a man's yard, Cotgrave 1611.

DINAH is leading SPEED *towards door 1.*

Don't love. Don't leave me. The children –

DINAH. They'll come with us.

SPEED. You needn't ever watch Loobie Loo again.

TED. There's such a thing as loyalty. I've been loyal.

DINAH. So many of our miseries come from holding on for duty's sake . . . being loyal to your family, your parents, your class, God, country –

SPEED. My old man, strutting about, saluting the flag, not knowing why.

DINAH. Haven't you always told me that? Loyalty's a killer, we must learn to change. Isn't that what your plays said?

TED *has grasped* DINAH *by both hands and is on his knees before her.*

TED (*desperate*). Don't, don't go –

DINAH. Let's make the break before it dies, Ted, while we still feel some vestige of affection for each other.

Suddenly she pauses and recoils.

Oh, no, what a shit you are! (*To* SPEED:) D'you know why he's trying to hold us here? I know that desperate look. He's got us in a scene he doesn't know how to end. I'm not staying here to be used.

She goes with SPEED*, door 1.* TED *gets up, as the lights come up. He* *looks at the page in the typewriter, tears it out, studies it.*

TED. She was right not to like being used as fodder. Some women might have liked it but she saw it as betrayal.

He crumples the page, drops it into the basket. He takes up another, reads.

TED. She knew he'd never laid a finger on April, May or June but he'd betrayed her in public, from Helsinki to Hobart once a night with two matinees. Not that she'd ever leave him for that kind of indecent exposure. She never doubted for long that he needed her. Certainly can't have gone on doubting after the opening of Miles's play.

He puts a page in the typewriter, sits to write. He types a few words as DINAH comes back by door 1, dressed for day, carrying some newspapers.

DINAH. I got three bai-joves and two gorblimeys.

TED. Are they any good?

DINAH. Look, they haven't even been opened. I picked them up on the way back from taking Becky to the coach for her school journey to Bodiam Castle.

TED (*reading a bai-jove*). Headline: 'Pink Champagne. Few playwrights of any epoch would dare bring together such disparate elements as Miles Whittier does in his dazzling comedy *Starboard Home*. Mahatma Gandhi, Rudyard Kipling, Anton Chekhov and Nellie Melba meet on a P & O liner, bound from Bombay to London. Soon they are ordering magnums and, in a classic drunk scene, concoct the peach and ice-cream dish that finishes by slipping down the Australian prima donna's ample bosom'.

DINAH. Headline: 'Look Back at Anchor . . . Book now for the cruise of a lifetime, a voyage so vivacious you'll curse your luck if you're not aboard . . .'

TED. 'Nor is the intoxication merely alcoholic. His dialogue sparkles like vintage champagne'.

Door 1 opens and ACTOR ONE comes with a handful of cuttings, reading. TED goes door 2, unnoticed by DINAH.

ACTOR ONE. More, I've brought more! Headline: 'Magnum Opus. What the last twenty years have been merely promising, Miles Whittier delivers'.

DINAH. 'Take the wife, take Aunt Edna, who must by now be ready for a few discreet four-letter words and a little tasteful nudity . . . it will make her proud to be British and she may die laughing.'

ACTOR ONE. '. . . so spellbound by his shimmering wordplay that we were hardly ready for the sudden depth, the sound of a heartbeat as strong and tender as Chekhov's own'.

DINAH. This one is a bit iffy. Headline: 'Not on your Nellie! . . . what's it all about, Miles?'

ACTOR ONE. That's a gorblimey . . . they don't count. (*He reads:*) 'Word-spinning brilliance. Wilder than Wilde – an Oscar winner' . . .

DINAH *and* ACTOR ONE *exchange a look of disgust. She notices that* TED *has gone, looks for him.*

'He had us reeling from the theatre, our feet on the pavement, our heads among the stars, glad to have been one of the privileged few at this once-in-a-lifetime marvel . . .'

DINAH. I think they're all right, Ted, don't you?

ACTOR ONE *goes on reading reviews.*

I'm going to ring him up and ask him if he thinks they'll be good for business. That's the main thing, isn't it, whether they'll sell tickets? Put the bums on the seats, isn't that what they call it?

She dials a number.

ACTOR ONE (*to her*). Those were only the bad ones. 'A Peach of a Play . . . "Aye aye, sir." murmurs the drunken Kipling, retrieving a spoonful of ice-cream from Melba's cleavage, "all shipshape." At which the Mahatma adds helplessly, "And Bristol fashion."'

We hear a lavatory flush and TED *returns with head wet, wiping face with towel.*

DINAH (*to the phone*). Hullo, Miles? Have you seen the papers? They look pretty good to us . . . He says they look pretty good to him too . . .

She looks round, towards TED.

D'you want to speak to him?

TED *shakes his head. She sees his state.*

Whatever's wrong? (*Into the phone.*) I'll ring you back, Miles.

She puts down the phone.

TED. I've been sick.

DINAH. I was so excited by the papers I didn't even see you go. Wasn't there any warning? No premonition.

TED. None at all.

DINAH. Your temperature's high. We all ate the moussaka the day before yesterday, and last night at Luigi's we both had the spaghetti vongole so if that's it why are you the only one?

TED. It's not food poisoning. It's bile.

DINAH. You brought up bile? A thickish fluid, either golden-brown or greenish yellow . . .

TED. Christ, woman, it's spleen!

DINAH. Now calm down, Ted. Bile comes from the liver, and it's hardly likely you've ruptured your spleen, not just by typing anyway –

TED. It's choler, gall! Not something I ate but something I read.

ACTOR ONE (*reading to himself*). 'If you can keep your head when all about you are rolling in the aisles' –

TED. It's not my spleen that's ruptured, it's my ego. My self-regard's had a sickening blow.

Canned laughter now burst out on the front-of-house speakers. TED *goes to the side.*

Who ordered laughter? I didn't ask for laughter at this point. What's there to laugh at?

DINAH. Darling, why don't you go and lie down. I'll draw the curtains and get you some Entero-vioform –

TED. Bed, curtains, for fuck's sake! Will you burn these papers?

He seizes and tears up The Times.

DINAH. Mind – that's got my crossword in it.

TED. Will you turn the clock back ten minutes to the time before I knew?

ACTOR ONE. 'Miles ahead!'

TED. Get off! (*Makes for him.*)

ACTOR ONE. The middle-Eastern stop-over is sheer Turkish Delight. A Look Back in Ankara –

TED. Piss off!

ACTOR ONE runs into the wings.

Will you turn the clock back ten minutes to the time before I knew? Before they all decided Miles is champagne to our cocoa? Can you give me back my innocence? My peace of mind?

DINAH. You can, surely, if you want to. You wrote it. Tear up the scene as you're tearing up those papers. Here.

She pulls the page from the typewriter and offers it. He pauses, sorely tempted.

TED. No. I couldn't tell myself that lie. It's a fact of life. He went out there an unknown and he came back a star.

DINAH. Aren't you happy for him?

TED. I wish him dead.

Canned laughter and applause. He glares out front, then at the wings.

Not funny!

The sound instantly stops.

DINAH. If you're determined to behave like a spoilt child, I've no patience with you. Let me have the crossword and come to me when you're fit to live with.

She goes, door 1, with The Times *in pieces. He opens the cupboard on another month on the girlie calendar.*

TED. April, May, whichever you are, you won't desert me, will you? Fairest on the wall . . .

ACTRESS TWO is JUNE, *a brunette in bridal veil and the bodice of a white gown but below the waist there's no skirt, only suspenders, white stockings, high-heeled shoes. She looks demure, carries a bouquet.*

ACTRESS TWO. In June we see a bride in bloom,
  Marrying the perfect groom –
  Not a has-been soured by gall
  But one who's running with the ball!

*She steps out, taking his hand. The 'Wedding March' is heard.
Another door slides open to show* MILES WHITTIER *in a morning
suit. Confetti falls through a rosy audience.* ACTOR ONE *returns,
throws streamers, takes flash pictures.* MILES *extends his hand to* TED,
stepping into the room.

MILES. Ted, I owe it all to you. How can I ever thank you?
  Without your constant help and unfailing faith in my ability,
  I'd never –

TED. Get off! Go on. This play's about us, not you. You may
  have taken over everywhere else but this den, this study, this
  theatre's mine.

ACTOR ONE. Gorblimey! Leave it out, Ted. Big smile!

MILES (*resentfully*). Not even as though you gave me a decent
  speech. Not a single joke.

TED. Write your own jokes. You can take April, May and June
  away from me but not this play. In this you shall be a total
  frost.

JUNE (*to* MILES). Don't answer. He'll only make you say
  something boring.

ACTOR ONE. Impossible!

JUNE. Miles admired you, looked up to you. How d'you think he
  feels to see you so embittered?

TED. I think he enjoys it. He can either be loved by his friends or
  the rest of the world. He can't have both.

MILES. No? Just you watch, matey!

ACTOR ONE. Hold that.

  TED *slides the doors, shutting out the music and cheering, but not before
  some dry ice has escaped into the room. Otherwise it looks as it did.
  He stands dazed until sounds of sheep, birdsong, tree-saw etc., fade in.
  He comes down, looks into the stalls through binoculars.
    A knock on the door and* DINAH *enters.*

DINAH. You ready for lunch? Earlier than usual as I've got
to get off soon after to meet Tom and Becky from the
London train.

TED. Right.

DINAH waves away some of the dry ice vapour.

DINAH. I hope you haven't spent the whole morning
in a dream?

TED. I must be going mad. I could swear those sheep have been
driving the dog.

He puts down the glasses, turns to her.

Anything happen in the real world? Anyone call?

DINAH (*showing video cassettes*). The Three Choirs Video Van.
You were tapping away so I didn't disturb you. I hope these
are all right.

TED. As long as they're total Hollywood crap.

DINAH. The driver recommended them.

TED. That's good enough for me.

He takes and looks at them.

TED. Ah, yes. *Wars in Space*. (*Hollywood trailer voice:*) I am the
envoy of the Throb of Organ.

DINAH. That sort of thing. How's the novel coming on? I want
something decent to read.

She tries to read what's on the page but he stops her.

TED. Novel? Ah. I did three pages.

DINAH. Good.

TED. Not good at all. I tore them up.

DINAH. Then what's that? Another fantasy about me and the
au pair boy? Not that I wasn't flattered. Did you really
think Speed and I were at it like knives? I mothered him a bit,
that's all.

She kisses him as he sits at the desk.

TED. A limerick. (*He takes the page from the machine and reads.*)
    When Shakespeare was stuck on a play
    Quoth he: 'I have nothing to say'.
    'Let's to bed,' his wife told him
    And there she consoled him.
    Whoe'er hath a will hath-a-way.

He throws it into the basket.

DINAH. Don't. That wasn't bad.

TED. I write a great many piss-takes but they're all thrown out.

DINAH. Parodies lost?

TED (*suddenly angry*). It's too late for laughter. I'm a man in
    middle age, living in a mean time. Remember what Santayana
    said: 'Fun is a good thing only when it spoils nothing better'.

He fetches a book of quotations, looks them up.

'No one is more profoundly sad than he who laughs too much'
    – Richter. 'There is nothing so illiberal – or so ill-bred – as
    audible laughter' –

DINAH. Hah! Who was that?

TED. Lord Chesterfield. 'Gentle dullness ever loves a joke' –
    Alexander Pope. 'Jokes are the epitaphs of the emotions'
    – Nietzsche.

DINAH. 'Laughing always comes to crying' – Ivy Parsons.

TED. Who?

DINAH. My Aunt Ivy. For fear we'd start enjoying ourselves. It
    was her life's philosophy.

TED. Laughing always comes to crying? Not bad. It's like what
    happens in my plays after the interval.

He puts down the book and they go out together.

ACT TWO

The front cloth as before with its projection of the manor house. House lights to half. TED *enters on the forestage, catching the audience short.*

TED. Once more, sweet gentles, welcome to the play!
    Half closéd eyes and moon-struck smiles bespeak
    A happy interval with grain and grape
    Til dread announcement harried you from thence
    To see Act Two. Lights out!

And they go.

                          And whoso wish
    To sleep in blest invisibility
    I give you joy. Yet, pray you, do not snore
    Lest 'mongst the mass be found some precious few,
    Some starveling band who came to hear the play,
    Whose pardon now I crave when they cry all:
    'Why limps our author so in leaden feet
    Through verse that's blanker than a virgin sheet?'
    No more ado; give ear; this doggerel bark
    Is his attempt to be Miles Whittier.
    Whiles you caroused in stalls and circle bar,
    This self-same popinjay became a god,
    By critics, actors, public, worshipped quite;
    His praises sung in halls of academe,
    His anthems rung in every counting-house.
    Come, sirs, e'en *you* bow down. You'd not be here
    Except you failed to get into *his* play.
    And in New Amsterdam, Big Apple called,
    A guild of scripters 'warded him the bays
    Best Foreign Dramatist, a prize he shared
    With Aeschylus. They got two votes apiece,
    Poor Shakespeare coming second-best with one!
    Sooth, *Miles* is biggest apple of the crop,
    Ripe Cox's Pippin to our bruiséd crabs,
    Sweet, juicy, yea, but rotten at the core;
    Parasitic, grafted to old stock,

Adulterate mongrel, bastard, water'd ale,
With filching fingers picking better brains.
From Swan of Avon, Stratford's livelihood,
Plucks he a quiverful of feathers bright;
From Monsewer Molière a *jeu d'esprit*;
From sallow Chekhov snatches he a sigh;
From Oscar gay, prim Shaw and Beckett dour
He draws his dues, a rent-boy on the make.
His betters' flowers mulch his compost-heap
Whiles cock-a-hoop he struts the midden vile
And crows his cackle: Whittier-than-you!
Meantime poor Ted, whose accents few can bear,
Thought he would imitate the one-vote Bard,
Go ape like Miles. But fie! Tis not his game.
He cannot mimic like a chimpanzee.
Ted Forrest's tone of voice, though oft-times cracked,
Is yet his own! Let's start the second act.

Exit.

*The picture of the house closes in as before and now the lights come up
behind and the scrim flies.*

*The Study is now a Breakfast Room, his desk set with a tablecloth and
cereal cartons, juice, coffee pot, etc. His typewriter is at the left side,
phone at right.*

*DINAH sits by the phone at right end. On upstage side, BECKY
(now 13½) and TOM (11) are sitting, eating breakfast, reading comics.
DINAH sips coffee and browses through* The Times.

*This sitcom tableau is prefaced by sitcom music, which fades when
they talk.*

Canned laughter is heard on jokes. TED comes in, door 2.

TOM. No, you didn't. I'll bash your face in.

TED. That's nice, I must say. The first thing I've heard you say
this morning.

TOM. She said she did a Great Exhibition when she was at
primary school but she's a bloody liar, ain't she?

BECKY. I'm not, am I, Mum?

TOM. Yes, you bloody are. And a shit.

TED. Now that's enough language.

TOM. You put it in your plays. Worse than that.

BECKY. That's different. That's for money.

TED looks for help to DINAH but she's starting to do the crossword. He sits at the left end and pours cereal into a bowl.

TED. In any case, Becky, you're not long out of primary school yourself. Only a year.

BECKY. Two years.

TED. As long as that?

BECKY. You don't know anything about us so don't keep butting in.

TED. Whatever gave you that idea?

BECKY. All right. Give you a test. What's him and his friend Aziz doing for their Great Exhibition?

TED. How should I know?

DINAH. Ted, honestly! He's been talking about nothing else for days.

TED. Right. I'm sorry. I've got a lot on my mind.

DINAH. Miles Whittier.

TED. *And* my anal fissure.

DINAH. That's only a symptom of Whittier syndrome. Like your heart attacks and nose-bleeds and urethritis and chronic hiccups and diarrhoea and constipation –

BECKY. Must we have this at breakfast? Uergh . . .

TOM. All about sore bums . . .

He makes a farting sound into his bowl.

TED. All right, tell me, what *are* you and your friend Aziz doing for the Great Exhibition project?

TOM. A great big picture of Disraeli in milk bottle-tops.

BECKY. Really boring. Honestly.

TOM. It's not, it's brill, so there. Stupid cow.

TED. It doesn't sound boring to me. It sounds brill. But then I'm not talking down from your great height in the first year of senior school.

BECKY. *Second* year! And it's a comprehensive school. Honestly! I'm 13 right?

Shows her T-shirt.

When I'm 14 I'll start working for my GCE, right? GCE means General Certificate of Education –

TED. I know what it means!

DINAH. Did you manage last night's homework?

BECKY. Didn't have any. It's double I.S. this morning and there's never any I.S. homework.

Pause while they all eat and drink. At last.

TED. OK. Is somebody going to tell me what Double I.S. is when it's at home?

BECKY. Integrated Studies. A double period. Honestly!

TED. And what does Integrated Studies mean?

BECKY. Oh, nobody knows that. Only what it's called.

TED. Thought so. Educational jargon. Mumbo jumbo. Should be got rid of. I might write to the head about it. Give him a piece of my mind.

DINAH. Waste of time. Old Jacko. He loves jargon. Don't you remember how he tells you a child is stupid? He says he's 'encountering difficulties'.

BECKY (*to* TED). Any case you're supposed to be writing TV plays, not letters.

TED. True.

TOM *has taken* BECKY's *comic. She smacks him, struggles.*

TOM. I was only lending it. You can lend mine.

DINAH (*absently*). Borrow.

TED. There you are. All that jargon and they haven't helped our son grasp the most elementary principles of English syntax. I say: get rid of it.

TOM. Get rid of you. You're boring. Boring old fart.

He makes the same noise into the bowl. TED *is struck by a memory.* TOM *and* BECKY *have swapped comics and* TOM *skims through.*

TOM. Oh, great! They've put Doctor Who instead of Jesus.

TED. You've broken my dream. I was being got rid of. In my coffin being buried.

BECKY. What would *happen* if you died?

DINAH. He isn't going to die.

TED. No, it's got to be thought about, now these heart attacks are getting worse.

DINAH. They're wind. Take up jogging.

TED. Anyway, I'm glad Becky cares enough to wonder.

Caresses her affectionately. She flinches.

BECKY. Have you made a will? I mean, what if you both died?

TOM. Yes, in a car crash.

He makes suitable sound effects.

DINAH. My sister and Uncle Les would look after you.

TOM. What about the car?

DINAH. I expect they'd sell it. They've got their own.

TOM. I want the car.

BECKY. What about your plays? Who gets those?

DINAH. I've already divided them between you.

TED. You've what?

DINAH. With the solicitor, yes. You were there. You signed the paper.

TOM. Don't want a lot of old plays. Gonna be a racing driver, not an actor.

DINAH. But when somebody puts them on you'll get part of the money people pay to see them.

BECKY. What d'you want to tell him that for? I could have had them *all*.

TOM. That's not fair, I didn't know.

TED. Nothing's fair in this world, Tom –

BECKY. Give him *Rotten Row*. That's your worst play, isn't it?

TED. No.

DINAH. Dad thinks it's his best.

BECKY. The one no one liked but you.

TOM. That no one ever puts on.

TED. That's the one.

BECKY. Let *him* have that one.

TOM (*angry*). That's not fair. I don't want that rubbish one.
I want *Beasts of England*.

BECKY. I've got that. Let him have *Going Dark*.

TOM (*to* DINAH). Is that a rubbish one too?

DINAH. You've got five each so stop arguing.

TOM. That's not fair. I want some TV plays. The funny ones
you're doing now. With us in when we were kids.

DINAH. Yes, you could have three each of those.

TED. If I ever finish them. At the moment it looks as though I'll
have to return the money. They're not funny at all.

DINAH. They will be when the laughter's added on.

Laughter. Front door-bell off. DINAH *stands, clears breakfast.*

DINAH. There's Sheila with Bill –

TOM. In her Volkswagen.

He makes car noise and moves out with a screech of tyres.
BECKY *stands.*

DINAH. I gave you your dinner money, didn't I? And, Tom, your
football boots are in the lobby or you won't be going to the
field. Becky, you're riding after school so don't be late home.

TOM *goes out.* DINAH *puts all trace of breakfast on a tray, leaving
only* The Times *and* Mirror.

BECKY (*to* TED). Riding. That's when you get up on a horse and
it moves along?

TED. Ha ha. Goodbye, both of you. Have a good day. Kiss
for Dad.

They go out, ignoring him. DINAH *takes his bowl, so that all he keeps
of the meal is his coffee mug. She goes out, door 2.*

Over this the sitcom music returns. When it fades, TED *has moved to the armchair, sits, reading a script he finds there. Lights have changed to their 'present day' state.*

Not bad at all. No wonder they turned it down. Of course, a novel wouldn't have canned laughter or closing music . . .

He puts down the script.

Also too much dialogue in a book is cheating.

The sudden roar of a jet-plane over the audience. It's as loud as the speakers can make it and brings TED *down to the front, staring out.*

Bastards! Bastard Yankee vandals! Scared the poor horses shitless. Look at them, galloping up the field.

He grabs the binoculars, looks. DINAH *comes in door 1, now wearing country overcoat and hat, goes to turn down the volume on the answerphone at the bookshelves.*

DINAH. I'm off to meet Tom and Becky from the train now. If you can't write, you can mulch around the beds and fruit trees with compost –

TED. About all I'll be writing is another bit of purple prose to that outpost of the Pentagon complaining about their bombers nearly blowing off our roof. Five hundred feet they're supposed to keep but that one nearly hit a mole.

DINAH. I've turned down the answering machine. Do *not* take any calls, especially from people you don't know. There may be some response to the news you died two years ago.

TED. Christ, I'd forgotten that.

DINAH. There's no point renting an answerphone if it's not used to cut us off and keep the world at arm's length.

TED. How can I keep the world at arm's length when every day at this time 'H' for Hank comes screeching across my lawn?

DINAH. The double-glazing men will be here tomorrow doing what they can about that. Did you forget that too?

He nods.

Is there anything you want from the chemist's? I'm calling in.

TED (*still looking through glasses*). Strychnine. Cyanide. Hemlock.

DINAH. Plant some seed if you've got the time.

DINAH goes.

TED. She used to look to me for seed. Now it comes mail-order in little packets.

TED returns to the script on the chair, reads, then brings it to the table and sits at the typewriter.

In a novel I can do without dialogue altogether. Deal with it in one paragraph of prose. In theory it should be liberating not having to express it all in talk. They none of them need speak at all if I choose. Then why doesn't it flow? Why am I blocked? Come on, tell the story. Describe his state of mind.

He reads the script and adapts it aloud.

'Some mornings during his mad spell, he managed to reach the papers before his wife could warn him. He knew only too well that if he sipped that delicious poison, the day was lost but as long as they were in the house he could never resist their terrible allure . . .'

Music. Light Change. He reaches towards The Times *on his desk. DINAH comes in, door 2, bringing the breakfast things back on the tray. She's as she was in the previous scene.*

DINAH. I shouldn't if I were you.

TED (*startled, withdrawing*). What?

DINAH. I shouldn't read The Times.

TED. Bad news?

DINAH. Pretty bad.

She sets out breakfast again, moves the paper from him, sits opposite.

TED. What?

DINAH. I'm not telling you.

TED. I don't mind so much if you *tell* me. I don't like finding it.

DINAH. And you can find his name if it's hidden among the financial news.

TED. As it often is. I could find it down a well. I scan a page and it's in Dayglo. I hear it across crowded rooms. I feel it as the princess felt the pea.

DINAH. Why not let me cancel the papers?

TED. Why not?

DINAH. Because he's on the list.

TED (*puts down the phone*). Ragtag?

DINAH (*to the audience*). Ever since she's seen the paper, Dinah had been expecting the phone to ring and to hear Alice Tail's voice, gloating over how poor Bob was on the way up again. Writers, she thought, were all the same: not the free, generous spirits their readers hoped, but envious, spiteful, treacherous, arrogant and cringing.

TED. Only the nicer ones.

DINAH (*to him*). The one man who's been decent and always treated you with respect is –

TED (*joining in*). Miles Whittier, yes, I know . . .

He doubles over in pain.

God, this ulcer's playing up.

DINAH. Eat some bran. No use killing yourself. Do something abstract. (*She reads a clue.*) 'Oliver's abandoned redhead'. Six letters. Third one's B. What Olivers do you know? Cromwell, Hardy –

TED. Goldsmith? It's Auburn.

DINAH. Auburn. *The Deserted Village*. Abandoned redhead yes, thank you.

TED. Did you know he was of an envious disposition? Made no bones about it either. Boswell argued with Johnson that they ought not to be angry with a man who was so candid.

He gets Boswell and reads.

'Nay, sir,' said Johnson, 'We must be angry that a man has such a superabundance of an odious quality that he cannot keep it within his breast but it boils over.' But Boswell goes on: 'In my opinion, however, Goldsmith had not more of it than other people have but only talked of it freely.'

DINAH. So it's nothing new? Salieri, of course, and Mozart.

TED. Yes. And Rimsky-Korsakov was so envious of Tchaikovsky he couldn't compose for years. Till Tchaikovsky died, in fact.

DINAH. Of course, it can't have been as bad in those days. At least Goldsmith didn't have Melvyn Bragg.

TED. That's true. Bach didn't have telly.

DINAH. He had Telemann.

The phone rings. They stare at it.

There she is. Alice Tail.

TED. Don't answer it.

DINAH. I can't just let it ring. It could be about the children.

TED. We must see about one of those new answering contraptions. You can choose who you talk to.

DINAH. It's no use.

TED. I'm on location in Ireland. Steven Spielberg –

DINAH (*into the phone*). Yes? . . . Oh sorry if I sounded sharp. I was expecting someone nasty . . . I'm not sure whether he's still in bed or on location in Ireland . . .

TED. I'm writing *The Throb of Organ*.

DINAH. Your father.

She gives him the phone.

TED. Dad? . . . anything but a good morning here but never mind . . .

DINAH. Even Walter was preferable to Alice Tail, thought Dinah, as she cleared the table. At least he didn't read *The Times*. Since Mrs Forrest's death the old man had lived in a twilight home with regular grand tours of the homes of his adult children. Of course they did their share. She quite enjoyed his visits, though for Ted they were purgatory.

TED *has finished talking, puts the phone down. She's cleared things onto the tray.*

TED. Our turn's come round to have him stay.

He takes the tray from her and goes, door 2. DINAH *speaks to the audience and clears the desk; spreads a green baize cloth over it. It's now a billiard table.*

DINAH. Their moves every few years into ever larger houses were all part of the son's efforts to impress the father. Boys start competing as soon as they're off the breast, she reflected over the washing-up. No wonder they love kissing nipples. It takes them back to a time before they had to fight.

She goes, door 2, as ACTOR ONE *comes on, door 1, as* WALTER. *He opens the cupboard door, finds cues on a rack and a marker. He comes down to look at the table and check that the balls are correctly set. Lights concentrated on the table.* WALTER *is in his 60s,* TED *his 40s.*

WALTER. Your brother Harry's doing wonderfully, son. Say what you like about the government of the day. They look after prison officers right enough. My Lord, yes. Guardians of law and order.

TED. That what Harry is? I thought he was a psychopath. Will you call?

WALTER. Heads.

TED (*tossing*). Heads it is.

WALTER *chalks his cue and breaks. There are no balls but we hear all the sounds of a real game.*

(*To us:*) In television plays these days there's always a snooker scene, thought Ted. *And* one on a railway platform with a steam train coming in. *And* a hunt ball with a hundred extras in period dress. A way of spending the money that might otherwise have gone on a decent script.

WALTER. Your stroke, son.

And as TED *breaks:*

My Lord, yes. Wall-to-wall carpeting, young Harry, not an inch of board showing. Wouldn't suit you. Eye-level microwave, quadrophonic stereo. Electric rotissomat on the patio. Rumpus room for the kiddies. Foul stroke, four to the old man.

TED (*angrily, scoring on the marker*). Yes, I know!

WALTER. I've brought some slides of Tarquin romping about with Wolf. Magnificent beasts, Alsatians. Wouldn't suit your tabby.

He pots a red, chuckles with delight.

Shot, sir! That was a matter of spotting a plant amongst the pack of reds.

TED. That's one of Harry's favourite tricks. Spotting a plant amongst a pack of reds. Last time we met he read me a lecture about my daughter linking hands at Greenham Common.

WALTER. This baize needs a flatiron over it.

TED (*to us*). Never hears what he doesn't want to.

WALTER. Simple safety shot then. Course it's years since I played.

TED. You'll never go to heaven.

WALTER. Yes, I'm proud as Punch of Harry. And your sister. Did I tell you Eileen was voted one-parent-family of the week for the whole of her area? I'm not saying *you've* not done well, son. This house may be a bit old but you're doing it up in your own way. Wouldn't do for Harry, of course. He likes everything just so.

TED knocks a ball off the table onto the floor. WALTER has lit a cheroot.

Too ambitious, trying to screw. You're not up to a screw yet.

TED replaces the ball on the table.

TED. Must you fill the room with that filthy stench? You know I can't abide the stink of cheap cheroots. It's like a recent cremation.

WALTER. Four to me! Not many pleasures left to the old man these days.

He waves smoke about but goes on smoking.

TED. Why not? Don't I give you enough money? If you want a rise, say so straight out. I'll mention it to my company treasurer.

He moves the position of the cue-ball while WALTER's back is turned.

WALTER. Isn't that Dinah?

TED. Yes. How much d'you want?

WALTER. Nothing, son. I'm very grateful for all you do. It's not that . . .

TED. What then? Your stroke.

WALTER. Haven't made it easy for me, have you? Ah, well – (*Playing.*) You don't seem to enjoy yourself like Harry and Eileen. Your sister's got far less than you in material ways, going out to work in a hotel kitchen to keep her darkie kiddie, but she has the inestimable gift of happiness.

During this they go on playing without score.

It's like your mother and I. We couldn't claim to have made much mark on the world, always living in digs, sailing close to the wind but through all our hardships, we never had a cross word.

TED (*incredulous*). What?

WALTER. When people talk about the Good Old Days, they don't mean material wealth. Look at you, with all yours – enormous old barn in a very *à la* part of London, dentists and advertising men among your neighbours, billiard-room –

TED. Not bad for a corporal, eh?

WALTER. You've been very lucky.

TED. No, I'm very talented and I've worked far harder than you did. Small wonder you never had an inside bog. You were bone idle.

WALTER. I'm not denying you've earned it.

TED. You were *about* to.

WALTER. But has it made you happy, son?

He marks one more. TED *cheats again.*

Poor Dinah doesn't know how to help you. All you care about, she says, is this man Whittier.

TED. She told you that? Disloyal cow!

WALTER. Don't blame her, son. She'd had a few of my Bloody Mary's.

He looks at the table.

TED. Made with *my* bloody vodka –

WALTER. Don't remember being snookered. She says you never think about her and the kiddies.

TED. Kiddies? Becky's nearly seventeen, about to leave school.

WALTER. Jealousy, jealousy, she says, day in, day out. She has to hide the papers or cut out the bits about *him*. Look what she's done to my *Daily Mirror*. In case you spotted it.

He takes from his pocket a lattice-work newspaper.

TED (*grim*). Spotted what?

WALTER. I couldn't see it mattered –

TED (*urgent, demanding*). What, what was it?

WALTER. Only that British Rail have named a train after him.

TED (*appalled*). A train? The Miles Whittier Inter-City?

WALTER. No, a Pullman. On the Brighton line.

TED. The line is immaterial!

WALTER. I thought you'd have seen it on the news.

TED. I never watch the news since they showed his waxwork in Tussauds.

WALTER. Well, they had him cutting the ribbon at Victoria. Seems a bit steep because, on that 25-part radio series of his life story, he said he'd never travelled on a train since the reviews for his first play. How's yours going, by the way?

TED. There's no Edward Forrest Pullman. Not even a goods van.

WALTER. Play, I mean. The one about your mother and me.

TED. It came off six months ago. And it wasn't about you, just two other boring mediocrities.

WALTER. Twenty-two to me and you've yet to taste blood.

He scores while TED *miscues, rolls a ball into the pocket with his hand.*

TED. They're giving it an award. The play you didn't know had come off for lack of bums on seats. *Going Dark*. Six for the blue.

WALTER. Five. All about people dying. There's enough of that in life. That's why your plays don't run, boy. Still, you got another prize. You'll be able to use them as book-ends. You always were a good prizewinner. Remember at school how the teachers loved you? Yet here you are racked with envy of other men. Whatever makes you behave like that?

TED (*mimicking*). 'What's this son? In your report? Still not top? But you could be – '

WALTER. Who's that supposed to be?

TED. 'And think how that would rile those toffee-nosed sods who blackballed me from the Masons'.

WALTER. That supposed to be me?

TED. Verbatim.

WALTER. Using words like that? Never. You were always prone to language.

While WALTER's chalking his cue, TED cheats again but this time WALTER sees.

You moved the cue-ball with your hand.

TED. I did nothing of the kind.

WALTER (*appeals to the audience*). Now did he or not? Be fair.

Cries of 'Yes', etc.

TED (*to them*). Scabs!

WALTER. If he tries again, you'll tell me, won't you, boys and girls? Whyever would you go to those lengths to beat your poor old dad?

TED. Because of you. I feel literally sick, my jaw aches with misery when I lose, my eyes fill with tears, the world goes dark. You passed on your sense of failure to me and I'll do anything to win.

Suddenly he strikes the floor with his cue.

I must kill him, that's the answer.

WALTER (*alarmed*). What?

TED. He's taking over, threatening to wipe the hero out entirely so I'll kill him off.

WALTER. Who?

TED. Whittier.

WALTER. I thought for a second you meant Yours Truly.

TED. Oh, I can kill you too. As Shakespeare did Mercutio.

Or when they wanted more Falstaff. Conan Doyle with Sherlock Holmes.

WALTER. But those people were fictitious. I'm real.

TED. That's what they *all* say. You're a character now in my television series and remember what happens when some old salt gets caught in a cottage.

He gestures slitting throat.

WALTER. You wouldn't do that, son. I've told them all in the car maintenance evening class to watch it and see what you've made of your dad.

TED has been to his filing-cabinet and fetched a script. He now advances on WALTER, threatening to tear it up.

TED. Mrs Proudie. Little Nell! The first mate in *Drifters*.

WALTER makes for door 1 and through it, shouting:

WALTER. Dinah, your hubby's lost his reason. Wants to kill his father . . .

TED slams the door on him, comes down, looking at the script.

TED. He'll do. He's not half bad. Thought Ted.

He puts it back in the cabinet, continues down to us.

He remembered Mrs Proudie's death. How Trollope had overheard two hurray Henries saying Mrs Proudie was boring, boring, so he went straight home and killed her off. The writer's privilege and revenge. Would Miles's death help Ted to a better life? Or would he become the first playwright martyr? *Saint* Whittier! He decided to risk it and began to devise an execution as glamorous and public as his life.

He opens the cupboard to reveal rows of cut-out statuettes, misted with dry ice. Lights on them as TED goes off.
   Music: 'Chinatown My Chinatown'. Strong applause.
   ACTRESS TWO comes from the wings in a gorgeous evening gown, bringing a stand-up microphone. After placing it, she applauds towards the side as though a prize-winner had just left. As it subsides:

ACTRESS TWO. The Best Supporting Actress In A Play

Translated From A Language Outside The Indo-European Group. The next presenter will be presented by the Most Honourable The Marchioness of Milton Keynes. My lady –

ACTRESS ONE comes on as a royal, wearing a gown and tiara. Slight applause.

ACTRESS ONE. My lords, ladies and gentlemen, the next presenter and I first ran into each other on the royal yacht *Britannia*, where – as always – his charm and wit kept the table on a roar. We soon discovered a mutual passion for riding and many's the time he's come and shot my husband's private shoot. A young man whose brilliance is only equalled by his modesty, who has won this very award for every play he's written so far – are you there, Miles?

Music: Zadok the Priest. 'May He Live Forever'.
    Spotlights search the theatre and find ACTOR TWO *as* MILES *coming from the stalls. He crosses the bridge between there and the stage and, as he steps to safety, it collapses. Unaware, he moves towards the royal. A sandbag or wrecker's ball drops from the flies, narrowly missing him as he steps upstage to bow to the* MARCHIONESS. *Cheering and applause reach a climax as he stands at the mike trying to subdue it. At last he bows as* TED's *voice cries from the front:*

TED. Fire!

A burst of rapid fire and the row of awards goes down. MILES *is unhurt.*

Geronimo!

Two arrows strike the set. ACTRESS ONE *is about to hand the award to* MILES *when she's struck by a third arrow and falls dead.* ACTRESS TWO *wrests the award from her and hands it to* MILES, *then returns to her place and drinks from a glass of water. She seizes her throat and falls, poisoned.* MILES *at last silences the crowd and the sounds of battle.*

MILES. In the days when I was struggling with my first plays, I looked with envy at the man who is about to add this scalp to his collection.

TED (*from the front*). It's yours I want! Where's the poisoned gas?

MILES (*not hearing*). And to his command of oxymoron dialogue, his mastery of domestic discord, his unique way of showing how an empire could fall because someone got a burnt breakfast. But I'm treading on thin ice here –

TED. I wish you were –

MILES. In danger of palming off on him a meaning he never intended. For wasn't it he who said, when asked where he stood on some issue of the day, 'Well back'?

TED. No, it wasn't, does it sound like me?

MILES. And remember his answer to someone who asked what his play was going on about. 'About 7.30 with a 3.00 matinee.'

TED. On the contrary I believe plays should have a point to make –

MILES. And who's to say he's wrong to refuse to deliver a message? He's not British Telecom. In the old plays, it was an occupational hazard of messengers with bad news to have their tongues torn out.

TED. That's one I didn't think of.

MILES. I only agreed to be your postman today because the news I bring is so good I know you'll only cheer. It's that the best play of the year is *Going Dark* by Edward Forrest.

Music: 'When I'm Sixty-four'. TED comes, wearing an old army greatcoat and helmet. The steel ball swings across again but MILES comes to meet TED and it misses. TED and MILES shake hands, the award is handed over and TED raises the statuette above his head to bring it down on MILES. He holds it by the marble plinth and when the statuette hits MILES's head it crumples like paper and he doesn't feel a thing.

TED. It isn't bronze at all. Cheap plastic rubbish.

He runs at MILES, who is by now at the side, applauding. MILES dodges the attack and runs off, chased by TED. Sitcom play-out music and a chase through strobe light. ACTRESS ONE has crept away. ACTOR ONE comes down, now as the critic.

ACTOR ONE. At the very moment when his hero should have denounced the whole fustian affair, the author had no lead in his pencil. He fell back instead on puerile slapstick. We asked for bread and we received a custard pie. Many scenes ago we had been promised an end to laughter, canned or otherwise, but still Forrest seemed unable to wipe the grin off his face. Funny perhaps, but where was the boo-hoo? A question answered in the nick of time with a long overdue touch of pathos. We learnt that his father was dying and went with the author to the old folks' home where he'd had his stroke, though –

ACTOR TWO *in a white tunic wheels on an invalid chair and helps the* CRITIC *into a dressing-gown.*

– even at this solemn moment, he could not resist sending him to West Sussex on the Miles Whittier Pullman.

He sits in the chair as WALTER. ACTOR TWO *covers his legs with a blanket then goes off.* DINAH *enters in nursing sister's uniform, with* TED *in an overcoat, holding a bouquet of spring blooms.*

SISTER. D'you know, Mr Forrest, they're having the time of their lives here. I nearly had a revolution just this morning. And why? Because they're not allowed to use foamy bath oil in the Jacuzzi. It's for their own good. They could drown in all those bubbles and we might not even notice.

And now to WALTER, *very loud.*

Visitor to see us. Your son the prize-winner.

They stand in his view. His head rises slightly and he stares at TED.

TED. Hello, Dad. How you keeping?

SISTER. Oh, nice and cheerful, aren't we? Mustn't get down in the dumps. That's not allowed, is it? Shall I put these flowers in water for you?

She takes them. TED *pulls a stool closer to him.*

He's done his duty so he should be all right.

She goes with the flowers.

TED. Dinah sends her love. Says you're to get well soon and beat me again at snooker.

No reaction from his father throughout.

You remember Dinah? Used to be a nurse? She was coming with me but couldn't leave Becky on her own. Your granddaughter, remember? The one with *anorexia*. Well, they've all got *anorexia* in her class. Quite the rage. Prevents them having periods, they tell me. A way of not growing up. Dinah says it's claiming our love and protection and I must

demonstrate my love more openly – but if I try to cuddle
Becky she tells me to piss off. Anyway, she kept her home to
feed her up a bit. Tom's doing his O-levels, but he's coming
down tomorrow. They sent these cards. Tom's drawn a picture
of your Honda. And this is from Dinah –

A pool of water appears under WALTER's *chair, spreading on the stage
floor.* TED *gives up.*

All you ever did was fight. All your life, thought Ted, though
even now he couldn't bring himself to say it aloud. It was only
when he got the old man in a play that he could speak out.

SISTER *returns with the flowers in a vase and puts them on the desk.*

SISTER. We all sat down and watched you win your prize. You
made such a nice little speech, I thought.

TED. There was a lot more I should have said.

SISTER. No. Some of them go on too long and try to be funny,
I said to Staff 'It's overkill', but you just thanked the actors
and smiled and were very nice. We were proud of him, weren't
we, Mr Eff?

TED. He's done his duty again.

SISTER. Dear oh dear – and after we promised Sister faithfully
we'd be a good boy.

TED. How did he promise if he can't speak? Now he's weeping,
look!

SISTER. No. Big boys don't cry, do they now? Their eyes might
water when they're a touch off-song but . . .

She's rung a little bell. She dabs his eyes.

TED. Stop pretending. He's not a child but a father of three and
a grandfather of four more. Fought in Burma. Did his duty.

SISTER. And now drives a Japanese car? Well, I never !

TED. How long's he got?

SISTER. We don't talk like that, if you don't mind. We try to
look on the bright side. Don't we, naughty boy?

ACTOR TWO *comes on as an* ORDERLY, *mops up the pool while*
SISTER *wheels* WALTER *in the chair towards the ottoman.*

TED. All his life the old man had fought, reflected Ted, as he sat in the train, eating the grapes there'd been no point in giving him. First with *his* parents, then his wife . . . Ted himself, his brother, and sister. The Masons. The Japanese.

SISTER. Oops-a-daisy!

The ORDERLY *goes to help the* SISTER *and they seem about to use the ottoman as* WALTER*'s bed but suddenly* SISTER *opens the lid and they bundle him into it like laundry. Then both go, with the chair.*

TED. And what for? A death scene without dignity. Without even a line. Then oops-a-daisy. It would have been too easy, he thought as he read over the scene, to write a last-minute reconciliation.

ACTOR TWO *comes on,(Door 1) as* TOM, *now aged 17.*

TOM. He said when he was a boy they used to sprinkle the streets with sand at funerals to soften the sound of the horse-drawn hearse.

TED. You didn't fight him, did you?

TOM. No. I really liked him.

ACTRESS ONE *returns as* DINAH, *a cloak over the* SISTER*'s uniform. With her:* ACTRESS TWO *as* BECKY, *black clothes with '19' on her T-shirt.*
    DINAH *takes the flowers from the vase, stands beside her husband and son. Dry ice mist surrounds them. They all face front.*

DINAH. It was on the first stroke of midnight he had *his* second.

BECKY. A day or two later. Before we could get down to Sussex to see him.

TOM. *I* got down.

BECKY (*angry*). All right!

DINAH. Sssh . . .

ACTOR ONE *has come on, no longer* WALTER *but a* VICAR. *He brings a bible and stands at an angle to the audience; a sly survivor.*

VICAR. The scenes of his father's death certainly brought a long overdue tenderness but, sad to say, too late. This might have been a most affecting valediction, a Look Back in Bognor –

TED. Who asked you?

TOM. Dad looked a right wimp at the funeral.

TED. I had a nasty moment when the box went down and we threw our flowers and handfuls of earth on the lid. I imagined I was in the box instead.

DINAH (*taking his hand*). It's all right –

BECKY. Everyone does that, OK? You like to think you're special but you're not, right?

VICAR. Instead the funeral became a mere pretext for trickery and for yet more petulant bickering.

TED (*touching the Bible*). Your lines are all in there.

VICAR (*pettishly*). Man that is born of woman hath but a short time to live and is full of misery.

He continues droning this beneath the following.

BECKY. I reckon just about everyone thinks: 'Christ, that could be me in that box'.

DINAH. You mustn't think that, darling, you're too young.

BECKY. You know that wally that wrote the fairy stories – Hans Christian Andersen? He was so scared of being buried alive, he made his mates promise to cut an artery before they nailed him down, OK?

DINAH. Now don't upset your father.

BECKY. Why not? He upsets everyone else.

DINAH. That's his job.

VICAR. Forasmuch as it hath pleased Almighty God . . .

BECKY. And when Hans Andersen went to sleep at night, he used to leave a note on the bedside table.

TED. What did it say?

BECKY. 'I only seem dead.'

TED takes out a notepad and pen.

VICAR. . . . . we therefore commit his body to the ground . . . earth to earth . . .

He sprinkles earth on the floor.

DINAH. Don't be so morbid, both of you.

TED. No, it's very good. Thank, you, Becky.

He makes a note.

BECKY. What's so good about it? He sounds a right wanker.

TOM. Why don't you shut up and listen?

BECKY. I suppose I've given him another scene now?

TED. Well, *part* of a scene. Near the end of the sitcom series.

BECKY. The ones with us in?

DINAH. They're very good.

BECKY. And I don't know why you have to protect him and bolster his ego. And dress up in that uniform because he's funny for nurses. Can't you see that's degrading? Exploitative?

DINAH. I don't mind if the sight of me like this helps put the lead back in his pencil.

BECKY. You'll be getting up like a land girl next. Isn't that another of his wet dreams?

VICAR. I heard a voice from heaven saying unto me, 'Write'.

BECKY. And every time you submit to one of these male fantasies, you become more of a hostage, right? To his demands, OK?

TOM. I just think you shouldn't have worn it to Grandad's funeral.

VICAR. And lo, he wrote and in the beginning found favour with the multitude and many that were there left off coughing and reading programmes and harkened unto him. But alas! the scribes gnashed their teeth saying amongst themselves; 'Reckoneth this man that we were born yesterday?' And it came to pass when the cocks crew that these same scribes, even as the fowls of the air, shat upon him from a great height –

TED (*to him*). You never miss a chance, do you?

BECKY (*to* DINAH). Why can't you stand up for yourself? Don't you care that you always finish up in one of his stupid plays? What about you, Tom?

TOM. I thought we'd come to bury Grandpa. And you couldn't even get down to see him before he died.

TED. She had *anorexia*.

BECKY. It wasn't *anorexia*.

TED. What was it then?

VICAR. Lord have mercy upon us.
   Christ have mercy upon us.

TOM. Right Dad, d'you fancy a drink?

TED. What? Is it over then?

VICAR. Lord have mercy upon us.

TOM. Sounds like it. I saw a pub on the corner with a pool table.

TED. No fear. You're too good for me.

TOM. Never improve if you don't compete.

TED. Don't want to improve. Only enjoy.

   BECKY *goes and they follow.* DINAH *remains with the* VICAR.

VICAR. The grace of our Lord Jesus Christ.

DINAH. In our day, when periods stopped we couldn't blame it
   on *anorexia*. It hadn't been invented. Becky doesn't know that
   we first met when I was a nurse and Ted was convalescing. For
   more than a week he'd been begging me to help hasten his
   recovery and the last bed bath I'd given him had been almost
   too much for both of us. The night before he was discharged,
   under the blue light, behind the screens, I climbed under the
   sheets and had my way with him. No wonder the starched
   linen, black stockings and smell of ether still turn him on.
   Long may they do so.

   VICAR *has stopped praying to listen to her.*

VICAR. World without end.

BOTH. Amen.

   They go together as lights come up, TED *comes on and we are back in
   the study on the day we began with.* TED *resets the props on his desk.*

TED. Once their children were off their hands, their daughter
   touring the slums with her Trotskyist theatre group, Scab
   Pickers or Pig Stickers . . . their son evading the Job Centre by
   going to university, there was no good reason for Ted and
   Dinah to stay in London. They bought an old manor house in
   Herefordshire. They seldom left the village, though took no

part in its life. They read no papers and Dinah bought her
crossword puzzles in book form. The mail was mostly offers of
golden toilet-roll holders and investments in Japan. When his
plays were put on here and there, old friends could be relied
on to send him any bad reviews . . . his agent would sometimes
ring to tell him his series had been turned down yet again.
Then Ted would spend some days rolled up in a blanket in a
dark corner. Dinah worried for his mental health. He pruned
the roses, manured the leeks. A portrait of the artist as market
gardener. He was happiest without hope, when life was as
close to death as he could manage.

The phone rings. He stares at it.

Still he couldn't quite resist the thought that his luck would
change.

He goes to turn up the machine.

NANCY'S VOICE. Oh, not this ghastly machine! Ham sandwich,
are you there? Alice!

TED (*automatically*). Dinah.

NANCY. Or even Ted.

TED. I can't face another rejection, Nancy.

NANCY. Very well, if you won't answer . . . some Yank's been
on the phone to say he's putting his attorneys on to
you because he's heard you're alive after all. What *does*
he mean, darling?

TED. I only seem dead.

NANCY. Thought you ought to know. Byeee!

*He has taken out a bottle of Scotch from the cabinet. He switches to
'record' and speaks.*

TED. This is Tom, only son of the late Ted Forrest. My mother,
still grief-stricken by my father's death, has gone on yet
another widow's cruise. If you wish to leave her a message,
please speak after the tone.

*He presses the tone button, turns the switch to 'receive'. The sounds of the
country swell during this: mainly sheep. He yells at the audience.*

Belt up, you brainless bags of wool!

The bleating increases, the phone rings. After some time, the machine answers with TED's *message.*

As soon as the call's over, I'm coming out there and if that row goes on, I'll be passing amongst you with the mint sauce.

We hear the tone, then the incoming caller. The voice is that of an embarrassed girl trying to do her professional secretary thing.

ACTRESS TWO (*voice off*). Oh, well, it's Mercia Television speaking. Sorry about your father. Ahm. Actually I'm ringing to ask where to send the scripts of his series, now they've been rejected. Whether to return them to his agent or direct to him. Well, his wife. Widow. Perhaps you could let me know. Hope the cruise helps. Cheers.

During this, he's taken the shotgun and checked that it's loaded. Dialling tone. He drains the glass, refills it, turns the knobs of the machine to cancel the tell-tale flashing light. Mimes opening French windows between him and us, comes down, escapes through audience with bottle and gun.
Door 2 opens and ACTOR ONE *comes on.*

ACTOR ONE. And so we came to the sad moment when the playwright made his escape through a pair of – wait for it – French windows! The man whose first exhilarating dash from the kitchen sink had been by 68 stairs into the sexy streets of Swinging London now reached into his threadbare prop-basket and pulled out that stand-by of Rattigan, Coward, Priestley and Maugham, glass doors onto a garden.

TED (*from the audience*). That's right. Back to the bog where you belong!

ACTOR ONE (*shouting back*). And not even the reversal of their usual places – playwright among the audience, critic on the stage – did much to blow the dust off this flyblown survival of Shaftesbury Avenue.

ACTOR ONE *exits, door 2, slamming it behind him. Door 1 admits* BECKY *and* TOM *in combat gear and casuals. She's about six months pregnant. He's smoking.* DINAH *follows, wearing the coat and hat in which she left to meet them.*
By their T-shirts we know BECKY's 20, TOM's 18.
TOM *takes the binoculars and looks over the audience.*

DINAH. Can you see him? He should be out there somewhere.
Muck-spreading.

TOM. Sort of busman's holiday, right?

DINAH. No, he doesn't write like that anymore, Tom. He hates
filthy talk these days. And all that sexual writhing on The Box,
I have to tell him when it's over so he can look again.

BECKY. Doesn't write anything much now, does he?

DINAH. He's begun a novel.

BECKY. This part of it?

She shows DINAH *the sheet in the typewriter.*

There was a young playwright called Miles
Who suffered extremely from piles –
Piles of money
For being so funny
And rolling them all in the aisles.

DINAH *screws it up, throws it into the basket. Finds another, reads.*

DINAH. A nurse with a playwright called Ted
Once enjoyed herself hugely in bed
How bitter her cup!
He could not keep it up
And both of them wish they were dead.

She throws this out too.

Oh, dear! I think I'll change and help him. If he comes in,
don't upset him.

BECKY. What if he upsets us?

DINAH. He will try. You mustn't be provoked into blurting out
what I told you in the car. Tom, did you hear?

TOM (*examining the stereo etc.*). Yeah.

DINAH. What?

TOM. What?

DINAH. What mustn't you tell him?

TOM. Just about everything.

BECKY. She means about Mercia turning down his series.

TOM. He's got to find out sometime.

DINAH. But not yet. He isn't ready. A blow like that might finish him off. He's already spent one whole day up a tree with a month's supply of sleeping pills.

TOM. I'm dying for a drink.

DINAH. There's fizzy in the fridge.

TOM. Great.

DINAH. He's not allowed anything stronger, only a glass of wine with dinner.

TOM. Right. (*But he goes on rummaging.*)

DINAH. All part of his cure. He nearly went mad this winter. We both did but now he's mending, slow but sure, coming out of his isolation. He needs all the help we can give him.

BECKY. Needs a boot up the arse.

DINAH. Becky.

BECKY. Yes, Mum. He ought to be made to face facts.

DINAH. He does already. Whittier's more successful. Dad's a flop. He faces that.

TOM *and* BECKY *exchange looks.*

TOM. Not just more successful. Better. It isn't fair to make him believe he can beat Whittier. He can't. Dad's plays aren't a patch on Miles's.

DINAH. How can you say that?

TOM. It's true, Mum. Our drama society did one of Dad's. Well, it was easy, only four people in it.

DINAH. *Beasts of England*? That's the one you'll get a share of when we're dead.

TOM. What can I say except 'thanks for nothing'. Only about ten in the audience and five of them left half-time. Including me. I was really – you know, sad and embarrassed. I never told anyone it was by my dad. Then I managed to get into one by Whittier. Had to stand at the back, but it was worth it. Really funny, OK? But something behind it, know what I mean?

DINAH. There's nothing behind it. It's just – what does Dad call it? Undergraduate.

TOM. We *are* undergraduates, so perhaps that's why we like it.

DINAH. Becky, you're in the theatre. Tell him why Miles is so successful.

BECKY. It's because he's better, Mum. Tom and I agreed to say this to you on the train from London. We did one of Whittier's one-acters at drama school. I never mentioned it here but it was knockout.

DINAH. He's more successful because he's politically OK.

BECKY. No, that's only why *our* company won't do him.

DINAH. Because he sucks up to the right people . . . journalists and royals.

TOM. That's not it.

DINAH. And his name's so catchy. He's married that media woman . . .

TOM.
BECKY. No, Mum . . .

DINAH (*desperate*). It's the way he does his hair!

BECKY. It isn't, Mum. He's better. That's all it is.

TOM. I mean, if word gets out that he's my father, I do stand up for him, but let's at least drop the lies at home.

BECKY. We reckon it would be better all round if we all admitted it and then found a way of telling *him*.

DINAH. Don't either of you dare. D'you think *he* doesn't know? Deep down, of *course* he knows but he's not ready to admit it, not quite. One day, yes, he will, well, not directly but through one of his characters.

TOM. One of us.

BECKY. Or all of us.

DINAH. That's how he talks to himself. And that would be the first step towards saying 'I'm only average.' Towards admitting he's been lucky to have his plays put on at all. Then perhaps he'll learn to live without ambition and be grateful for any crumbs that come . . .

She can't go on, but subsides into tears. TOM *and* BECKY *confused, embarrassed.*
    BECKY *comes to console her mother.*

BECKY. Come on, Mum, it's all right.

DINAH. Tom, will you carry Becky's bag upstairs?

BECKY. I can carry my own bag. Christ, I'm not a cripple.
    I'm only pregnant, OK?

DINAH. Make some tea if you like.

TOM. It's well past teatime.

But DINAH*'s gone.* TOM *goes to the filing-cabinet and looks where* TED *found a bottle.*

Where's he keep the Scotch these days?

BECKY. She's no good for him, killing him with kindness. He'll
    be a basket case in a year or two.

TOM. In my class at sixth-form college, I was the only guy whose
    parents hadn't split years since. Talk about embarrassing. Still,
    we're only here the weekend.

He crosses to the shelves, looks for Scotch in drawers, plays with the answerphone.

I'm not looking for any aggro, know what I mean?

He turns on the message.

TED (*voice off*). This is Tom, only son of the late Ted Forrest.
    My mother, still grief-stricken by my father's death . . .

TOM. Christ, hear that? It's not a suicide note, is it? She said he's
    been talking about topping himself.

BECKY. He loves himself too much to do that. You notice he
    didn't take them pills when he was up that tree?

TOM. The gun. The shotgun's gone.

They move to look out front as a shot is fired behind the audience.
BECKY *mimes opening the window and runs to see.* TOM *follows. The* CRITIC *comes from door 2.*

ACTOR ONE. Oh, no. Not that! The arbitrary gunshot, the
    handy rope, the implausible precipice.

He too looks over the audience as TOM *and* BECKY *go down into the stalls.*

A device that was so thrilling in *The Wild Duck*, *Hedda Gabler*, *The Seagull*, *The Lower Depths* and *Six Characters in Search of an Author* seems in our time a mere Look Back with a Banger. A man who once contrived such exciting deaths for others might have done better for himself.

The lid of the ottoman is opened and TED *sits up inside it.*

TED. How about this then? He didn't go out into the garden. He got into the box. Is that better?

ACTOR ONE (*returning to face him*). No, it's even worse. A reversion to the cheap magic shows of his childhood. Trickery. Dramatic doodling!

The CRITIC *sits at the desk to write his review.* BECKY *returns as* TED *climbs out with the gun and bottle.*

BECKY. Mum said you were in the garden. We thought you'd done it.

TED. Too easy. No. I had to be in there all along and hear what you said to her.

BECKY. You just don't bloody care, do you? How much you scare us?

TED. My dear, of course I do.

He tries to kiss her but she avoids him.

BECKY. Piss off.

She sits on the box as he returns the gun.

TED. I *was* in the garden, then I saw it had to be the box. The coffin. I had to be reborn in there.

BECKY. Reborn? You lost your marbles or what?

TED. And now look. You're lying on it with my grandchild. It's all working out. (*To the* CRITIC:) I hope you're noticing this.

TOM *returns, mimes opening window, comes in.*

TOM. Might have known.

TED. Hullo, Tom. Aren't they open then?

BECKY. You talk as though he's a wino.

TOM. Takes one to know one.

TED. Never touch it these days. Not a word about this to your mother. You'll find a tooth-glass in the lavatory.

He shows the bottle.

TOM. Toilet.

TED. Sorry.

TOM. Cheers.

CRITIC. Cheers.

He means he wants a glass too.

TED. Your mother's taking ages with that change.

TOM. She can't decide on her next costume.

BECKY. My money's on the land girl.

TED *goes to door 1, opens it and calls off.*

TED. Dinah, I need your help. Don't take a moment longer than you have to.

TOM *fetches glasses from the WC.*

We're all in the study.

ACTOR ONE. Where else would they be, one wonders. As we draw to a close of this Look Back in Rancour, the problems of setting the action in one room become painfully apparent.

TOM *pours Scotch for each of them.* TED *shuts the door, comes back, seeing.*

TED. Just a minute. Drinking my Scotch? Buy your own.

ACTOR ONE (*having drunk*). In so many ways, the author seems to lack even the most elementary graces.

TED (*grabbing the bottle*). You pollute my toilet, rubbish my plays then have the gall to talk about grace.

ACTOR ONE. There's no pleasure drinking with a skinflint.

He finishes his glass and makes for door 2.

TED. You're welcome to a drink if you'll stay and help.

ACTOR ONE. If Forrest had written *A Christmas Carol*, Tiny Tim would have died of starvation.

He goes. TED *shouts after him.*

TED. Freeloader! (*Turning back.*) How can he say that? Only this morning I sent three cheques to charity. I'll bet *he* hasn't adopted an acre of African rain-forest.

BECKY. Great. Now you can spend an average weekly wage on dinner in a five-star restaurant.

TED. Not round here. The nearest is Worcester. We thought we might take you over there.

BECKY. And you make out in all your plays you want to change the system?

TED. Yes, change the system so every one can afford a five-star lunch.

TOM. She's winding you up, Dad.

BECKY. I just don't know how he can live with *all this* when he knows about *all that* – Ethiopia, Nicaragua, Bangladesh –

TED. Because I didn't want *all this*: 15 rooms, 4 baths, 2 acres, 81 chairs.

TOM. Forced it on you, did they?

TED. It happens, Tom. All I had when I was your age went into a suitcase. I only wanted the use of a hall. I wanted to change the view from the French windows.

TOM. That's about all you will change through plays because 99 out of 100 people never go near a live theatre and when they do they want girls got up as cats or trains.

BECKY. He's never wanted to change anything.

TED. I hunger for change. I sit staring out at the fields, dreaming the sheep have turned on the dogs. Flocks of them converging on Whitehall, covering Parliament and Palace in a great heap of droppings. Sending the royals to the Job Centre, suffocating the Stock Exchange in a blanket of wet wool. My pornography is news footage of revolution – Manila, Haiti, Cuba, the Winter Palace . . . I long to see Switzerland sacked, its bloodstained vaults thrown open, their software burnt on purifying pyres. You think I wouldn't be glad to lose my 81 chairs? If they came marching up the lane from Hereford, you think I'd fight? I'd meet them with open arms.

Trouble is, the guns. They'd have to have guns because most people in manor houses would fight to keep them. And how would they know I'm on their side? And as I can't stand pain and wouldn't want to see your mother shot, I think I'll await the democratic process.

BECKY. Oh, standing ovation.

TOM. You're both the same. Volvo radicals!

TED. Ah, yes, thank you.

He goes to write this down as DINAH *comes in door 1, dressed as land girl.*

DINAH. I thought you were in the garden. I was coming to help.

TOM. Lovely Linda.

BECKY. The lusty landgirl.

DINAH (*defensive at once*). You know very well I bought this outfit in the village jumble. I wear it for the mulching.

BECKY. You wear it for him. To please him.

TED. And you make an old man very happy. Or would if things hadn't gone so dark.

DINAH (*to* TOM). What have you been saying to him?

TED. Nothing. I knew about Mercia turning down the series.

DINAH. Oh, God, how?

TED. It doesn't matter. I'm glad it's off. They'd only have filled them with snooker games and hunt balls. No, it's worse than that. I know now what I have to do. I was in the box, staring at the lid, imagining it was all over. No series, no novel. So what's the way forward? I must turn them into a stage play.

TOM. Not again.

DINAH (*thrilled*). Of course.

TED (*takes in the audience*). Well, obviously I must have or we'd none of us be here.

He goes to shout at door 2.

But there had to be a moment when I thought of it. That's one of the rules – and I do try to stick to the rules.

DINAH. Why is he shouting at the lavatory?

TED. I do believe in the tyranny of form.

BECKY. All right for you. You're the tyrant.

DINAH. But this is wonderful. You should be over the moon.

TED. At what? D'you realise what this means? I've got to write it.

DINAH. Ted, you've broken through.

TED. Have you any idea how *hard* it's going to be? Cramming all our life for the last twenty years into one room?

TOM. With three walls?

TED. Exactly, and changing the scene without seeming to and making sure you all have your say –

TOM. Not me. Not going through this again. I'm off.

BECKY. Me too.

DINAH. How can you? Just when he needs you most.

TOM. Why should I have to stay here till he decides to write 'Exit Tom'?

DINAH. I'd have thought you'd *want* to help. It's Dad's plays pay your fees, your rent, your beer-money. And all he asks is that you talk to him now and then.

TOM. So he can copy down what I say? Then get me acted by some prick from drama school?

TED. Come on, son, another Scotch?

DINAH. Ted, you're drinking alcohol!

TOM. No, he's not. He's drinking coloured water. As you know. And this isn't his study and there's rows of people sitting out there in the dark – coughing!

BECKY. This sort of theatre's done for anyway.

TOM. Right. Ever since films came in.

TED (*to* DINAH). There you are. So that, even after I've got it down and found an ending, and Nancy's told me it's worse than my last, we'll still have to find some producer mad enough to stage it. And once it's on, what then? Enter Bronco Bill.

Door 2 opens; ACTOR ONE with cuttings.

ACTOR ONE (*cockney*). Gorblimey, Ted, pull the other. We're not so green as we're cabbage-looking. Reckon we can't see when someone's floundering? Splashing about, getting nowhere fast?

He rips off the page and gives it to TED. He sits at the desk and lifts the phone.

DINAH. Then why don't you help him? Don't just stand there watching while he drowns.

ACTOR ONE (*posh, into the phone*). Capital T The truth is that no one comma, least of all the critic comma, told him to jump in the first place full stop.

He pours more Scotch.

DINAH. What are you doing?

ACTOR ONE. Phoning in my copy.

DINAH. A bad review.

TED. Of my play?

DINAH. On our phone?

TED. On my Scotch?

ACTOR ONE. You didn't expect a good one?

DINAH *tries to take the phone or cut him off,* TED *tries to wrest the Scotch from his grasp.*

Capital I it has never been within the province of criticism to throw artists a life-belt full stop.

DINAH. Well, it is now – so start thinking.

She has cut him off and got the phone. TED *shows his fist.*

TED. You've always been so handy with 'what a shame' and 'if only' and 'where Forrest goes wrong'. Well, now's your chance.

ACTOR ONE. If any harm comes to me, my colleagues in the Critics' Circle –

TED. None of you leave this three-sided room till you help me end the play.

ACTOR ONE (*cockney*). Have a heart, Ted. There's pensioners sitting out there with last buses to catch.

DINAH. Then the sooner we help, the sooner they can go.

BECKY. It's not important, OK? These places are all closing down anyway.

TED. Going Dark.

BECKY. And it makes no odds whose plays are wittier – yours or Miles's. D'you think they care in Ethiopia?

TOM. They don't care a lot in London.

TED. Leave alone Offa's Dyke.

He appeals to DINAH.

So why should *I*?

DINAH. Whether anyone cares – that's a luxury.

ACTOR ONE. 'For us there is only the trying. The rest is not our business'.

TOM. T.S. Eliot.

The CRITIC *nods, surprised.*

DINAH. Do it for me. I care. If all the theatres are closed, we'd be into a new Dark Age. A whole world staring at screens that can't hear or see them. Where not even the laughter's real.

Canned laughter.

ACTOR ONE. Broadway is already The Great Dark Way.

TOM. Tell the truth, Dad, you can't do anything else. They didn't want your TV plays.

BECKY. They didn't want your *films*.

TOM. Written any good books lately?

DINAH. That's it. You didn't choose your work. It chose you. All of you.

TED. I know.

DINAH. There's no way out.

TED. And, of course there's no real ending. Only another start. Act one, scene one, The writer's study.

BECKY (*kissing* DINAH). Right. Now that's settled. I'm off to make some beetroot soup. And later on I'll pick some magic mushrooms up the Iron Age Fort, make you and Dad an omelette, get you stoned, OK?

DINAH. Thank you, dear, that would be nice.

TOM (*following* BECKY). Hang about, Becker, you still got that Thucydides?

BECKY. I might have.

TOM. Can I have a lend?

DINAH. Borrow.

ACTOR ONE. For what he's given us in the past, Ted Forrest has earned some indulgence.

He offers TED *his chair,* TED *sits.*

We can't expect a meat course every time and may have to make do with a trifle, a *jeu d'esprit*, a promissory note, a piece of his mind. As such –

He goes and DINAH *closes door 2 on him.* TED *puts a page in the typewriter.* DINAH *sits on the desk as the* NURSE *did in* TED's *dream.*

DINAH. I wish you'd talk to the kids directly. Why d'you always confuse them with irony?

TED. How else can I deal with their youth, vitality, good looks and single-mindedness? What else can I offer *but* confusion?

He types a few words.

DINAH. They hate you putting words in their mouths, making them despise you and say you're worse than Whittier.

TED. I could put him in here. Perhaps I can write him out of my life.

DINAH. Put your hand up my leg if it helps.

TED. Oh, I'm not starting now.

DINAH. No?

TED (*shakes his head, reads what he's written*). Revising a limerick.
   Even when they were burying Ted
   Dinah wouldn't believe he was dead.
   The lid of the coffin
   Kept sliding off him,
   His pencil was so full of lead.

DINAH. So when will you be starting?

She locks door 1 and goes to the ottoman, starts undoing her leggings.

TED. Tomorrow.

DINAH. No. Tomorrow Glazekleer are coming to put in your
   soundproof windows.

TED. Cutting him off still further.

DINAH. And that's the ending?

TED. Something of the sort.

DINAH. Not particularly happy.

TED. No. Funny boo-hoo.

DINAH. Even if he's isolated, can't hear or won't listen. Even if
   it's curtains for him, isn't there some way you can send them
   out with a song and dance?

*He bolts door 2, goes to her, switches on the typing tape and begins to
help her undress.*

TED. Easier said than done.

DINAH. That's where the fun comes in.

TED. I'll see.

*He stands by her as sounds from the outside world get louder: tree-saws,
church bells, cows and sheep. TED moves to embrace DINAH on
the ottoman.*
   *Lights dim and the gauze comes in. ACTORS ONE and TWO
return in overalls. Daylight. They examine imaginary glass between
them and the audience. One finds a speck and rubs it off with his
forefinger. The other polishes by breathing and rubbing with a cloth.*
   *DINAH's gone off. One of the workmen calls TED from the filing-
cabinet where he's finding his scripts. He inspects the windows. The
workman demonstrates, letting a white feather fall gently to the floor.
TED points out over the audience and we hear a jet fighter scream across*

but no one on stage hears anything. DINAH *comes with a mug of coffee and joins them. They suddenly strike a pose and move upstage.* TED *sits at his desk and begins typing, inaudibly. The cupboard doors fly open to reveal* ACTRESS TWO *as a showgirl. She goes into a rousing showbiz finale. She steps down into the room, helped by the men, and they all perform the number, well-rehearsed and carried out. They bawl the last refrain but we hear only the sheep.*